Pastoral Counseling

A

MINISTRY OF THE CHURCH

JOHN PATTON

Abingdon Press • Nashville

Pastoral Counseling: A Ministry of the Church

Copyright © 1983 by Abingdon Press

Second Printing 1984

Library of Congress Cataloging in Publication Data

PATTON, JOHN, 1930—
  Pastoral counseling.
  Includes index.
  1. Pastoral counseling. I. Title.
BV4012.2.P35   1983   253.5   83-3729

ISBN 0-687-30314-1

Some of the material in chapters 1 and 2 is adapted from "A Theological Interpretation of Pastoral Supervision" by John Patton, excerpted from *The New Shape of Pastoral Theology* edited by William B. Oglesby. Copyright © 1969 by Abingdon Press. Used by permission.

The excerpt on pages 109-10 is from *Openings into Ministry* edited by Ross Snyder. Used by permission of Exploration Press.

The dreams on page 221 are adapted from the article "The Dialectical Relationship Between Mystery and Ministry" by John Patton. Reprinted by permission from *Quarterly Review: A Scholarly Journal for Reflection on Ministry* (Fall 1981), copyright © 1981 by Abingdon and the United Methodist Board of Higher Education and Ministry.

MANUFACTURED BY THE PARTHENON PRESS AT
NASHVILLE, TENNESSEE, UNITED STATES OF AMERICA

To Helen

Acknowledgments

Writing this book has been a fascinating endeavor for me, most of the time, more play than work. This is not to say that it has been easy, just different, and to that extent re-creative. What I get paid for is doing things: pastoral counseling, administration, some supervision, and teaching. Writing is an extra that prior to now has been done only in bits and pieces, some articles or an editorial in the *Journal of Pastoral Care*. Writing a book has required a change of life-style: getting up early to do the writing, then getting out of my head and into my body through jogging a few miles, and after that going back to what I spend most of my time with—people.

I am indebted to many of those people for helping me with the writing: first of all, those to whom I have attempted to be a pastor, some of whose stories, in intentionally unrecognizable fragments, appear in this volume; to our office staff at the Georgia Association of Pastoral Care: Diane Wright, Glenda Halliday, Anne Greene, and Damaris Ramirez, who typed most of the manuscript; Calvin Kropp, pastoral counseling director and business manager, who took over my administrative duties for five months; the Board of Governors of GAPC, who granted me an "all-except-counseling" study leave for that same period of time; (pastoral counseling centers are seldom well enough financed to provide any other type of leave, and counselees seem to think that the things they are working on are considerably more important than a book); to my colleagues in the American Association of Pastoral Counselors, who have argued with me enough about some of the issues discussed in the book to motivate me to present my point of view in more systematic form.

A number of other colleagues and friends have assisted me immeasurably in providing criticism and comments on the manuscript. The book, whatever its limitations is far better because they read it and talked with me about it: doctoral students, Don Hartman and Jim Philpott; pastoral counseling specialists, Bill Boyle and Bill Johnson; professors, Shirley Guthrie, Ben Kline, Bill Mallard, Walt Lowe, and Herb Anderson; parish ministers, Garnett Wilder, Tom Conley, and Harry Beverly. Finally, I express deep appreciation to my colleagues on the staff of the Georgia Association for Pastoral Care, past and present, who have helped me learn that although there is no such thing as *pastoral cure,* there is *pastoral care.* And that may be enough.

Contents

Introduction

This is a book about what pastoral counseling is and how it is done. My task would seem simpler if I could choose to write about either the "what" or "how" without the complications of the other. That type of simplification, however, is deceptive and actually leads to further complication, for what pastoral counseling is is integrally related to how it is done. In fact, at least part of the reason for writing another book on this subject is the fact that too many people have assumed that any type of counseling done by a pastor is pastoral counseling, or, on the other hand, that in making use of knowledge and methods from the psychotherapeutic field, one ceases being a pastoral counselor and becomes a psychologist or a marriage and family therapist.

My concern is to claim for the practice of ministry all the psychotherapeutic knowledge that a pastor has the time or training to integrate into his or her particular ministry. I attempt to do this by developing a theory of pastoral counseling based on the pastoral relationship—something which those who have become specialists in pastoral counseling and those for whom this particular ministry is one among many have in common. A theory based on the pastoral relationship involves both the "what" and the "how" of pastoral counseling. It must state in a variety of ways, "In the light of what a pastoral relationship is, this is what pastoral counseling is and here is an example of how it is done."

Underlying this concern to develop a theory of pastoral

counseling which focuses on the centrality of the pastoral relationship is an effort to claim or reclaim pastoral counseling as an authentic ministry of the church. Whereas the direction of the pastoral counseling movement until very recently seemed to be away from the church and toward the practice of a secularized psychotherapy, there is strong evidence that it is moving back toward the religious community where it originated.

Pastoral counseling today is less likely to be a search for cheap psychotherapy than a personal quest related to religious and theological concerns. The pastoral counseling center has become a "halfway house" between church and world where such concerns can be discussed without having to identify with a particular religious community.[1] One could interpret this as either a defense or a direction. I see it primarily as the latter.

Another reason for writing about pastoral counseling in terms of the pastoral relationships of both generalist and specialist is that some of the main resources of the pastoral counseling movement have not yet been applied to this task. Much of what we have learned about the clinical method, the relationship between theology and psychology, and the issue of specialization within ministry has been used primarily in the training of specialists. Although this task is important and one in which I have been involved for over fifteen years, many of the most valuable things we have learned have not yet been applied to the basic understanding of the pastoral relationship. Concepts such as diagnosis, free association, transference, and the like are not only useful in pastoral psychotherapy, but have important implications for understanding and offering a pastoral relationship by both the generalist and specialist in pastoral counseling. Moreover, those who are beginning clinical training for a pastoral counseling ministry need to learn the more general implications of psychotherapeutic concepts for the pastoral relationships as well as practicing their more specialized applications.

Some time ago, Morris Taggert[2], in a study of the membership of the American Association of Pastoral

Counselors, raised the question of whether or not pastoral counseling was becoming a profession among other professions functioning in the health care field. He asked questions appropriate for identifying a profession and applied them to the field of pastoral counseling. For example, does there exist within pastoral counseling a body of knowledge, a point of view, a way of understanding human events that, although found among members of other professions, are represented institutionally within pastoral counseling—or does there exist a set of professional competencies related to the body of knowledge, for which there is a clearly visible educational process?

It may be that the leaders of the pastoral counseling movement in the early seventies wished to think of themselves as pioneers in the development of a new profession much as did Robert Holt who argued in the book[3] he edited in the same period that psychotherapy itself should become a profession. My own view is that pastoral counseling is a "subdiscipline" (a term used by Lawrence S. Kubie in an article in the same volume) and specialization within ministry. It is a function performed on occasion by all ministers and is an appropriate part of the education for general practice in the Christian ministry. It is also one of the ways in which a minister may choose to specialize within the profession of ministry.

The important concern for me is not pastoral counseling's status as a profession, but the way it can be practiced as Christian ministry. What, if anything, makes counseling pastoral? I do not intend to present a new method of counseling that ministers need to master in order to be effective. My concern, rather, is to integrate into a theory of Christian ministry some of those elements that have been a part of pastoral counseling training since the mid-fifties. There is one Christian ministry within which both parish minister and pastoral counseling specialist perform complementary functions. This book is written for ministers in both contexts for ministry. There *is* no one method of pastoral counseling that all ministers should learn. There are many methods just as there are many types or styles of ministry. There are many psychotherapeutic theories which can contribute significantly to the understanding of the human condition and methods which respond effectively to the pain of human life. In the midst of this diversity, however, some common understandings of pastoral ministry and pastoral counseling need to be stated in more systematic form.

Contributions of the Pastoral Counseling Movement

My conviction about this grows out of my own experience in the pastoral care and counseling movement during the past thirty years, first as a student and then as a practitioner. Although it is difficult to define what this movement is and is not, I believe that it can profitably be described in relation to three significant events: the emergence of clinical pastoral education as a significant factor in theological education in the late forties, the development of new professorships of pastoral care and counseling in the seminaries in the fifties, and the organization of the American Association of Pastoral Counselors in the sixties. Virtually all the pastoral counseling teaching and practice in the past thirty years has been significantly influenced by at least one, usually more than one, of these events and what they represent.

My first experience in clinical pastoral education came in the mid-fifties in a university hospital. As I reflect on that experience, what seemed most significant was the tremendous amount that can be learned from one concrete incident of ministry, how much more was going on than I was first aware of. After my second and third experiences I continued that examination of the concrete actions of ministry, but focused on the fact that it was *my* ministry and *my* person. I discovered that not just my action, but my whole being was involved. That central conviction of CPE (Clinical Pastoral Education) became one of mine: "You can't be a good pastor without looking at yourself in relation to what you do."

In a graduate program directed by one of the "new

professors" of pastoral care, I experienced something of the dialogue between theology and psychology. My favorite professor in college had been a psychologist who was also a minister, but this was different. Here in this new field was an attempt to integrate psychological understanding of personality change into theology, not simply to use psychology in the practice of ministry. Moreover, as in CPE, there was an interdisciplinary experience of learning with students in the behavioral sciences and theology who were studying human personality together. The fact that one can learn theology by reading psychology and learn psychology by reading theology became an important part of my thinking.

As a CPE supervisor and hospital chaplain in the mid-sixties, I became aware of the organization of the American Association of Pastoral Counselors and the "debate" between Seward Hiltner and Howard Clinebell as to the appropriateness of such an organization.[4] At first, I was negative or indifferent to the work of A.A.P.C., believing with Hiltner that pastoral counseling is something that all ministers do and that developing it as a specialty within ministry would ultimately separate pastoral counseling from ministry as a whole. I now hold a different view. More important, however, is the fact that the formation of A.A.P.C. has challenged the pastoral care movement to deal with the issue of specialization and its implications for the practice of Christian ministry.

These three issues, which I have identified with three successive decades of the pastoral care and counseling movement, will be evident throughout the book. The power of clinical material to raise questions about one's faith and practice which has been identified with the emergence of clinical pastoral education will be an important part of my method of presentation. The dialogue between theology and psychology is present in some way in every chapter. The questions raised by specialization for the general understanding of ministry and the contribution of specialized concepts, particularly from psychotherapy, to the more broadly conceived work of pastoral counseling will also be present throughout. These three issues make up an important part of the heritage of the pastoral counseling movement, as it has emerged in the last thirty years, and need to be claimed for the theory and practice of Christian ministry.

Far from having "cut the nerve of ministry," as an article in *The Christian Century* suggested several years ago,[5] the issues called to ministry's attention by the pastoral counseling movement serve to remind the church of its understanding of the human condition and the power of Christ's relationship to persons in the world to transform that condition. Pastoral counseling as a ministry of the church can enrich the church's understanding of itself and its mission to broken humanity.

Method of Approach

My particular concern, however, is with pastoral counseling, understood as Christian ministry, and what is involved in a theory of pastoral counseling that focuses on the importance of the pastoral relationship. Christian pastoral counseling may provide a variety of things depending on the needs of a particular situation, but its central feature is the offering of humanness in relationship which is in some way patterned after the humanness of Christ for us.

I use the term "relational humanness" as a normative concept for describing what pastoral counseling should offer and for determining whether or not a particular type of counseling can be understood as pastoral. I speak of relational humanness as normative for pastoral counseling in a way similar to Tillich's speaking of the term "New Being in Jesus as the Christ" as normative for systematic theology. A norm emerges, according to Tillich, in response to a particular apologetic situation and serves to criticize and correct all other components of theological construction.[6] The growth of such a norm

> is a historical process which, in spite of many conscious decisions, is on the whole unconscious. It happens in the encounter of the church with the Christian message. This encounter is different in

each generation, and its difference becomes visible in the successive periods of church history. The norm grows; it is not produced intentionally; its appearance is not the work of theological reflection, but the Spiritual life of the church.[7]

Similarly, relational humanness as a norm for pastoral counseling has emerged from that part of the church particularly concerned with the ministry of pastoral counseling. How this has occurred is discussed in the next chapter. Here I am attempting only to introduce the general structure of the book.

Relational humanness with a person or persons to whom one is attempting to minister is made possible and sustained by three active relationships or ongoing dialogues, which are discussed successively in the first three chapters of the book. The first of these is with the Christian story, particularly the story of who Jesus was and is for us. The second dialogue is with the role and function of the Christian minister. The third is with the community which authenticates one's ministry. These dialogues between or relationships with the story, the ministry, and the community are the principal criteria that make pastoral counseling pastoral.

In the light of the discussion of what pastoral counseling is, the book moves to some of the more important questions involved in describing how pastoral counseling is done. In successive chapters I discuss the questions of how one structures a pastoral counseling interview, how one determines the unit of care or the particular persons to be seen in counseling, and the nature of the diagnostic process for a *pastoral* counselor. In the last two chapters I deal with the questions, What heals in pastoral counseling? and What happens in the counseling process? These questions may be framed in a variety of ways, but they demand the attention of anyone who is seriously involved in a pastoral counseling ministry.

All that is said in the discussion of these questions is addressed both to the generalist and the specialist in pastoral counseling. They are the same questions which, in one form or another, have confronted seminary students, parish ministers, and experienced specialists in pastoral care and counseling. All three are involved in determining what pastoral counseling is and how one may offer it as Christian ministry.

Definitions

The meaning of the terms that I have been using will be clarified later, but some preliminary definitions are important at this point. Since "all ministry is a sharing in Christ's ministry, the many ministries of the people of God are one. (I Cor. 12:12-13). Each is a distinctive form of the single ministry of Christ."[8] *Pastoral care* is one of those distinctive forms, and it is understood here as the broad response of the Christian community through her ministers to persons who are in some way alienated from their faith or from other persons. The modifier, "pastoral," is a general reference to the church's care for persons through one of her representatives rather than a reference to the services offered by the administrator of a parish.

Pastoral counseling is a type of pastoral care which is performed by one who has been educated theologically for ordained ministry and who has the identity and accountability of a clergyperson. In pastoral counseling the roles of the primary giver and receiver of care are more clearly defined than in pastoral care, and the alienated person has taken initiative to seek the help which he or she needs. It may include support, guidance, and a variety of other means through which care may be expressed.

I continue to prefer the term "pastoral counseling" to that of "pastoral psychotherapy"[9] as the primary designation for this type of ministry because of pastoral counseling's closer relationship to the religious tradition. To be sure, many ministers, both in parishes and in more specialized settings, offer psychotherapy that is as good or better than that offered by those who are primarily health professionals. It seems more useful to me, however, to define pastoral psychotherapy as a more narrowly focused type of pastoral counseling that has been structured for the achievement of personality change and growth.

A *generalist* in pastoral counseling is one who understands his or her vocation to include pastoral counseling as a relatively minor part of ministry. Generalists may have competency in counseling comparable to their competency in preaching, but in terms of the time and preparation devoted to that particular ministry function it remains one responsibility among many. A *specialist* in pastoral counseling is one for whom counseling is the major expression of Christian ministry. Specialists continue to perform other ministry functions, but they are primarily committed to pastoral counseling. Furthermore, pastoral counseling specialists have training beyond the basic preparation for professional ministry that is designed to facilitate the specialized practice of pastoral counseling. Moreover, they have been certified as competent pastoral counseling specialists by a responsible group of peers who are practicing their ministry this way.[10]

Limitations of Perspective

The method of the book is influenced throughout by the issues that I identified as emerging from the pastoral care and counseling movement: the use of case material, psychological theory employed in the service of theology and ministry, and specialization in ministry influencing the way in which Christian ministry itself is understood and carried out. Some of the limitations of my perspective on pastoral counseling may have already become evident to the reader in the discussion of some of my personal involvement in the pastoral care movement. Others may appear later in the discussion. My understanding of theology and of pastoral counseling is strongly influenced by my experience as a white, male Protestant from the southeastern part of the United States. My experience in receiving care both as an individual and as a half of a couple, influences how I think about and do pastoral counseling. For example, many of the clinical illustrations which I use come from relationships with couples. This, no doubt, is because I have had many significant experiences on both sides of the counselor–couple relationship and because I hold the theoretical view that counseling of couples and families is pastoral counseling, not a new profession that a pastor may learn.

The reader will also note that I express strong opinions about certain issues, particularly about the practice of pastoral counseling. Although I have done a great deal of teaching and supervision, I am primarily a practitioner. I have spent a great deal more time doing it than thinking about it; therefore, some of what I say is clearly a description of what I have done rather than a careful presentation of theoretical possibilities. My hope is that the reader will take my sometimes opinionated views as a challenge to clarify his or her own rather than simply accepting or rejecting mine. I am less convinced that the things I say about what pastoral counseling is and how it is done are correct than that the questions I address must be addressed in some way by those who are seriously concerned about pastoral counseling and Christian ministry as a whole.

I turn now to a discussion of relational humanness as the norm for pastoral counseling.

Chapter One

Relational Humanness and the Christian Story

I now attempt to describe the meaning of relational humanness as a norm for pastoral counseling and the way the pastoral counselor's ongoing dialogue with the Christian story contributes to and sustains that norm. The concept of relational humanness comes from two sources: (1) experience in the ministry of pastoral counseling, both in the attempt to identify competent pastoral counselors and in experiences of pastoral counseling itself; and (2) interpretations of the Christian story, particularly the Jesus story.

The theological interpretations which I judge to be relevant to this task are obviously chosen by one who views the Christian tradition from the stance of a pastoral counselor, a stance that is informed by who Christ was and is. At the same time, experience in this ministry, which appears to be "meaning-full," influences what is seen to be most significant in the story. The story is never fully objective and free from my interpretation of it. There are, however, certain themes or central features of the story that appear so consistently in the various theological interpretations that they take on, if not an objectivity, an "over-against-ness," which makes genuine dialogue with the story a possibility.

In this chapter, I begin with the experience of one fragment of the Christian community attempting to identify authentic pastoral counseling. I move to an interpretation of the central elements in the story of Jesus as the Christ and then suggest how the humanity of Christ may be related to our humanity.

Finally, I present two case excerpts from my practice of pastoral counseling which, I believe, have been influenced by my dialogue with the Christian story. They are elements of my experience in ministry which have been perceived as "meaning-full," and which have been previously shared for critique and criticism by colleagues in the ministry of pastoral counseling. They serve primarily as examples of the type of experience I bring into dialogue with the Christian story. Later, specific details of the cases will be interpreted in the discussion of how pastoral counseling is done. I turn now to the first experiential element in the description of relational humanness.

The Community of Pastoral Counselors

An important part of being and remaining a minister is the actual practice of ministry and the attempt to identify genuine Christian ministry in oneself and others. For the pastoral counselor the identification of authentic ministry is most often done in groups of colleagues committed to the same type of ministry. The American Association of Pastoral Counselors is one of the ways a structure is provided for the meeting of such colleagues. One of the Association's many tasks is to find ways of recognizing competency in pastoral counseling. Through committees of persons who have specialized in pastoral counseling, the Association has found ways of determining levels of competency in this particular function. Although the members of these committees represent a variety of denominational and educational backgrounds, there has been a remarkable consistency of opinion in stating that a particular person was or was not functioning adequately as a pastoral counselor.

For ten years I participated in the deliberations of these committees, listening to recordings of counseling sessions, interviewing pastoral counselors and listening to them interpret their ministry both theologically and psychologically. As the process developed, I observed this community of ministers consistently asking certain questions as they interviewed candidates: Is this person present, alive and available to his or her counselee and to us as a committee? Is he or she able to use the counseling relationship as a means for learning and growth? Has the counseling process moved from talking about problems "out there somewhere" to experiencing them "between us" or within the relationship?

The deliberation of a community of pastoral counselors involved in identifying authentic pastoral counseling is, in my judgment, a significant part of the life of the church, from which, as Tillich suggested, a norm may develop. In the process of saying that a particular pastoral counselor is expressing authentic Christian ministry, the community experiences and celebrates that ministry. Moreover, something of what the Christ was and is is revealed. The community involved in identifying competent pastoral counseling is certainly not the whole church or the whole church as it should be, but it is an authentic fragment of the church which expresses the whole as it carries out its special mission.

Relational humanness is not a term chosen by any official committee of pastoral counselors. It is simply what seems to me to be a useful way to describe what the committees are talking about in their attempts to define counseling that is genuinely *pastoral.* And it can be, at this point in time at least, a central interpretive key or norm for describing what pastoral counseling is and is not. It does not come from one person or theory of psychotherapy or of ministry, but from a dynamic process of doing ministry and reflecting on it within a community of pastoral counselors. The values represented by the concept of relational humanness have emerged mostly unconsciously from deliberations on both what seems useful in ministry and on the source of that ministry—Jesus, the Christ.

Pastoral counseling does not develop apart from the faith and the church. Christian pastoral counselors attempt to offer ministry in continuity with who Jesus was and is, and they examine all theories and procedures for ministry in relation to a norm for pastoral counseling which is derived from involvement in the Christian community and dialogue with theology.

21

The key words here are involvement and dialogue. Although I am convinced that a norm has emerged which can assist us in determining what is and is not pastoral counseling, it is not an idealistic standard intended to challenge the pastoral counselor to continuing involvement in the community committed to Christ's meaning and to dialogue between experience and theology that wrestles with that meaning. Relational humanness as it has been experienced and described by the pastoral counseling movement can also be thought of as an interpretive bridge between contemporary experience and Christian tradition. Such bridges or hermeneutical keys are continually being developed by the church in order that Christian meaning may remain contemporary and relevant to life experience.

Dialogue with the Christian Story

A Christian cannot do ministry without—at least implicitly—addressing the question of the nature and character of the Christ whom he or she represents. At this point in history, what has been most clearly apprehended and affirmed about Christ as a result of the ministry of pastoral counseling is his humanness in relationship—a relationship that binds and challenges in order to offer freedom. This is not a reduction of Christ's meaning to that which is most clearly apprehended about him as a result of the depth encounters of pastoral counseling. It is, however, an affirmation that something of the Christ may be seen more clearly as a result of this particular dimension of ministry.

The relational humanness of Christ is a point of clarity within the total picture of him, which reveals features about him with a clarity unavailable when trying to keep the total picture in focus. The issue then is how to maintain this point of clarity without losing sight of some of the features essential to the whole picture. The process is not unlike the use of the "f stop" on a camera. One must make compromises between illumination of a particular feature and clarity of the whole field of vision of Christ as revealed in the Christian tradition. Our limited emphasis, while necessary and inevitable, must always stand in relation to the broader picture.

Peter Hodgson has described Christology as "present responsibility and as historical quest." Christology, however, "maintains continuity with the tradition often by means of the most radical discontinuity. We move backward only by moving forward." He quotes Ernst Käsemann appreciatively when he says that "continuity with the past is preserved by shattering the received terminology," and interprets that as meaning "we can say again what came to expression in Jesus only by saying it differently." In each epoch of the church's history Christology "has had to engage in a 'coherent deformation' (Merleau-Ponty) of tradition in order to maintain continuity with it."[1]

We do not have to pursue Hodgson's discussion of theological method further to see some of the implications for ministry which he mentions. People do not simply transmit what they have received. The message is inevitably *handled,* interpreted, and de-formed from the way it was heard and experienced. It is then re-formed and re-interpreted in a way that attempts to demonstrate its continuing meaning and relevance for life today. In discussing the picture of the Christ which informs pastoral counseling, I will be both continuous and discontinuous with the tradition, attempting to de-form and then re-form the story of Jesus, the Christ, for ministry today in a way which maintains continuity with what that story has meant in the past.

In order to do this, however, I must know the story and genuinely encounter its essential elements. Otherwise, some features that seem particularly congenial with a contemporary experience or point of view may be seized on and used to promote that way of thinking or acting. As an editor of a pastoral journal I have read, and consistently rejected, articles that attempted to justify some pastoral procedure on the basis of knowledge about the intentions of Jesus or some other psychological interpretation of incidents in the Gospels.

Claiming knowledge about another person's motivation, rather than finding ways to let that person speak for himself/herself, is suspect in contemporary psychotherapeutic practice. Such claims are even more dubious in dealing with historical documents. Coherent deformation of the New Testament story must continually attempt to avoid manipulation of it for one's own pruposes.

A pastoral counselor, or any other interpreter for that matter, cannot completely avoid such manipulation. And I do not claim to have avoided it in what I am attempting in this chapter. A person guards against such extreme distortion, however, by continually encountering the whole story. "Reading a story, whether the Gospel story or any other," says Hans Frei,

> has been rightly compared to understanding a work of visual art, such as a piece of sculpture. We do not try to imagine the inside of it, but let our eyes wander over its surface and its mass, so that we may grasp its form, its proportions, and its balances. What it says is expressed in any and all these things and only by grasping them do we grasp its "meaning." So also we grasp the identity of Jesus within his story.[2]

This is the importance of the ongoing dialogue with the Christian story for the Christian ministers who claim to express something of the story in what they do and say.

Although we cannot construct a biography of Jesus the way we can for other historical figures, we can construct a theological picture that will guide us in our efforts to bring our ministry into significant relationship with the ministry of Christ. In doing this, we must remember that what are "more important than the historically proved authenticity of a particular saying are the ruling tendencies, the peculiar forms of behavior, the typical basic trends, the clearly dominating factors, what is not pressed into schemes and patterns but the 'open' total picture."[3] This "open" total picture is what must be brought into dialogue with relational humanness as presented in the material from pastoral counseling.

Essential Elements in the Story

Obviously there is an arbitrariness as to what is perceived as "the total picture" of Jesus as the Christ. What it must include, however, if it is to be without major distortion, are the three major elements in the Christ event: his life, death, and resurrection. Many theologians have focused on these elements. It seems clear that any picture of humanity that is genuinely informed by the Christian message must in some way reflect all three. Langdon Gilkey sees in them, "a fundamental dialectic" characteristic of both the Christ and of human existence. There is a dialectic of affirmation, of negation and a higher reaffirmation that "in overcoming the negative, also transmutes the originating positive."[4]

Estranged history is transformed by the coming rule of God. In Jesus' historical life, for example, "if one would be first, one must be last; if one would lead, one must serve; if one would live, one must first die. . . . He is Messiah only as the weak, the vulnerable, the suffering, the disgraced, and the forsaken one; he is lord only as he who was crucified; he is saviour and giver of life only as he who was not saved and who died." Theology, says Gilkey, "has sought to interpret our existence and our history in the light of this baffling mixture of elements which together make up Christology."[5]

The first element in the dialectic of the Christ event underscores the relational nature of humankind. We have been created for community and for neighbor-hood. One of Jesus' parables, the good Samaritan, is central in the picture of who we are—persons who need and who need to respond to the needs of others. We are neighbors by nature, not simply by proximity. Jesus' own life and his response to other persons convey an affirmation that, in spite of its limitations, being human and being related by need to other persons is acceptable to God. Attempts at self-sufficiency and proving one's rightness are unnecessary and irrelevant efforts to gain approval. Jesus' own humanity is a statement that our human creatureliness is acceptable to God. In fact, the Kingdom comes not in some far off place, but in the midst of this kind of neighbor-hood.

The second element of the dialectic, however, reveals the depth of our estrangement from God and our identity as communal beings. Humankind reflects a continued denial of neighbor-hood; therefore, because of human brokenness and the pervasiveness of sin relationship involves suffering. To be human is to hurt. To be related is to experience the brokenness of relationships and vulnerability to an evil in relation to which we seem to have no power.

Within this second element of the dialectic, however, is the affirmation that has been the focal point of the Christian faith, the ultimate power of suffering love. Jürgen Moltmann has described this love in a relational (my term, not his) way—from the point of view of both the Son and the Father. The suffering of both is essential to the meaning of the cross. From the point of view of the Son, not only was there physical pain, but "his abandonment by the God and Father whose immanence and closeness he had proclaimed." From the point of view of the Father, there is the infinite grief of one who abandoned the Son to suffer death on the cross. "The grief of the father," says Moltmann, "is just as important as the death of the Son."[6]

> The Father suffers in his love the grief of the death of the Son. In that case, whatever proceeds from the event between the Father and the Son must be understood as the spirit of the surrender of the Father and the Son, as the spirit which creates love for forsaken men, as the spirit which brings the dead alive.[7]

Moltmann describes the intensity and power of suffering love, in effect, relationally, from both sides of the suffering. The cross addresses both abandonment and grief. The crucified God is near "in the forsakenness of every man. There is no loneliness and no rejection which he has not taken to himself and assumed in the cross of Jesus."[8] The relational humanness, therefore, which is placed in juxtaposition with the second element of the dialectic revealed by the Christ event, must be acquainted with grief, with loneliness, and with pain.

The third element of the dialectic points to the power of God to overcome even the final estrangement of death. Jesus' resurrection is an event "that participates in our ordinary existence but culminates and transcends it." It affirms that there is indeed a "higher reaffirmation that in overcoming the negative, also transmutes the originating positive."[9] Moltmann describes the resurrection as "the source of the risen life of all believers and as a confirmation of the promise which will be fulfilled in all." Through the working of the Holy Spirit one can have "a hopeful and expectant knowledge of this event" and enter into "the dialectic of suffering and dying in expectation of eternal life and resurrection."[10]

Moltmann sees eternal life as "hidden beneath its opposite, under trial, suffering, death and sorrow." Its hiddenness, however, is not simply a paradox but a latency which "presses forwards and outwards into that open realm of possibilities that lies ahead and is so full of promise."[11] A part of that promise may be the consolation of the beyond and hope in the future. Another significant part, however, is what Moltmann has described elsewhere as one of the "basic characteristics of the life of Jesus—making alive the frozen relationships between human beings."[12]

Essential to understanding the third element in the Christ event, therefore, is the recognition of the continuity of all three elements. The "Spirit which brings the dead alive" is the same Spirit "which creates love for forsaken men" and creates persons in neighbor-hood. New life in Christ involves grace in spite of suffering, not without it, relationship when relationship seems impossible, the experience of life when nothing is evident but death. It is a new life with nail prints and scars, one without complete healing. New life means the strength to go on in spite of a continuing brokenness. Community is reconstituted in the knowledge that the healing which has come is not an end in itself, but a healing which can enable persons to engage in their vocation of achieving God's

27

purpose of neighbor-hood. The reaffirmation that is achieved in the dialectic of the Jesus story is one in which mystery and suffering remain as characteristic of life in this world.

Relationship within the person of God and with humankind may be seen in Jesus' witness to neighbor-hood as the purpose of human living. It may be seen, further, in the relational suffering of Father and Son in the cross, and in the resurrection's affirmation of new life in spite of the power of sin and death. What is normative for pastoral counseling, if it is indeed in dialogue with the Christian story, is a pastoral relationship that is in some sense expressive of all three elements of genuine humanity which Jesus as the Christ revealed.

Analogia Relationis

I know of no more persuasive statement about the nature of humankind in the light of the Christian story than one made by Karl Barth, although I have difficulty with the way he claims to have arrived at his point of view. Barth's statement that we must "base our anthropology on Christology" seems to me to be essentially correct. I do not believe that it must be based "only on this."[13] Although he does not acknowledge it, much of Barth's understanding of humankind appears to be, like mine, based on his own human experiences as well as on biblical revelation.

According to Barth, rather than an *analogia entis* being between God and humankind, there is an *analogia relationis*. We are like God in our relatedness. The humanity of Jesus consists in the fact that he is *for* other persons. Humanity for Barth is fellow-humanity. We are with our fellows as Christ was for us. He continues, "The humanity of man consists in the determination of his being as a being with the other." Only the "humanity of Jesus can be absolutely and exhaustively described as being *for* man.[14] Other humanity is being *with* the other. Barth uses the pronoun, "thou," to speak of persons in relation, attempting to transcend the pronouns, "he," "she," and "it." One cannot be person without another person, an I without a thou.

The humanness of the encounter with another person in relationship is described as having four major characteristics. The first is *being seen* or being visible to the other. "All seeing is inhuman in which the one who sees hides himself, refusing to be seen by the fellow-man whom he sees." The second characteristic is *mutual speech and hearing.* "I and Thou must . . . speak with one another and hear one another. The "expression and address between I and Thou are reciprocal. As we can look past people, we can also talk past and hear past them." The third characteristic of humanness is *rendering mutual assistance.* "My humanity," says Barth, "depends upon the fact that . . . I need the assistance of others as a fish needs water. It depends upon my not being content with what I can do for myself, but calling for the Thou to give me the benefit of his action as well." Fourth, humanity depends on doing all of the above with *gladness,* or I would interpret this, with a kind of childlike openness. This is what Barth calls doing "all this in one's essence." A person "is only what he is gladly." "Man is essentially determined to be with his fellowman gladly . . . to chose not to do so expresses not his nature, but his sin."

> In its basic form, humanity is fellow-humanity. Everything else which is to be described as human nature and essence stands under this sign to the extent it is human. . . . Man is in fact fellow-human. He is in fact the encounter of I and Thou. This is true even though he may contradict it in both theory and practice . . . even though he may pretend to be man in isolation.[15]

What the pastoral counseling movement has seen as normative for a pastoral counselor seems surprisingly close in meaning to these statements from Barth. Although our sin may prevent us from being fully *for* others, it is possible to be relationally human *with* others. Training in pastoral counseling, at its center, is a process which experientially teaches persons about the nature and necessity of human relatedness after the manner of Christ. If we believe that human life is essentially neighbor-hood and denial of neighbor-hood is a real fact of life broken only by God's relational intervention in Christ, then any sharp distinction between saint and sinner, well and sick, normal and abnormal, is significantly less useful than a relational approach to the hurt of human living.

Pastoral counseling offers relationship and witness to the possibility of healing. If it is pastoral counseling, it cannot simply claim to offer healing. Healing in the New Testament is most often seen as a sign that the kingdom is at hand or that the Christ has become related to a particular human situation. Healing and revelation, Tillich has insisted, are inseparable. Healing through pastoral counseling, therefore, is a gift that may be discovered when God's relationship to us is revealed. It is not something that can be produced or achieved apart from it.

"Meaning-full Experience" in Dialogue

In the light of this understanding of the Christian story and of relational humanness as a normative concept for pastoral counseling, I turn to two excerpts from my experience in ministry. I do not attempt to interpret their meaning in this chapter. Some of that is done later. My concern here is to present the type of experience that is brought into dialogue with the Christian story and that has contributed to developing the concept of relational humanness. Experiences like these, which are perceived to be "meaning-full," contribute significantly to my interpretation of the Christian message, because they say to me, "This is what life is all about."

Joanne[16] is a thirty-year-old who was in pastoral counseling with me on two separate occasions. On the first occasion, a period of over a year, she dealt with a number of specific problems, such as, her unrealistic expectations of herself, disappointing relationships with men, and some of the familiar issues involving young adult separation from parents. She was not "cured" (I don't believe anyone ever is) but she was functioning responsibly as a program administrator for a human services agency. She came the second time for pastoral counseling to "try and make some sense of some things."

Although she was not depressed, she was anxious and still grieving over the slow agonizing death of one of her staff members. She recognized her fear of her own death and that of her parents and the loneliness of life. She seemed to be searching for a way for things to make sense. I have difficulty with Tillich's categorical distinction between existential and neurotic anxiety, but, descriptively, the focus of Joanne's anxiety at this point in her life was existential.

The week before the event I shall describe, Joanne told about a dream in which she was in Munich, the scene of her college "junior year abroad." Munich represented for her the time in life when she was "most alive." In the dream when she looked above the houses of the city, she saw sinister dark clouds that frightened her. It was misting rain, and as she looked around her, she saw old women carrying black umbrellas. The interpretation of the dream which emerged sounded like a Jungian dialogue with the shadow or Jacob's wrestling with the unknown angel. It was an exciting session.

This week, in contrast, Joanne was apparently depressed and fatigued. She couldn't get over a virus and was angry with her body, her physician, and implicitly with me. (I chose not to make an interpretation at this time.) It was wrong that she couldn't get well. She didn't know what was physical and what was psychological. She did not say, nor did I, spiritual. As she sat crouched in her chair, she again expressed her fear of death.

Aware of her tension and mine, I asked her to sit back in her chair, in effect to open up her body, and to express what she felt. In a few moments she began to sob uncontrollably and sometimes to shriek. I did not cross the room to comfort her. After a while, before the sobbing stopped, I asked her to try to put some of her feelings into words. She spoke of the unfairness of it all, of wanting to give up. She asked (I think well aware that I could not do that) for me to commit her somewhere. I said nothing, and then shortly afterward (as my own anxiety subsided) I recall that she said that although she didn't want her employees to know of her hospitalization, she feared "coming apart completely."

She gradually calmed down, and I reflected some of her feelings verbally, but mostly I became aware of my own sadness. I don't think at this point I knew what the sadness was about. It was clear to me that as she began to feel better, my own pain got worse. Although I was primarily aware of my own feelings, I was also aware that she was talking about my caring for her, how I was to her a "father, lover, and religious person." I remember noting that combination of symbols and the order in which she put them as she went on to talk about how important it was to her that I was a minister.

I made no interpretation of the transference or, more generally, what was going on in the relationship. Instead I shared with her a fantasy that had come to me as she had moved up out of her despair and began expressing herself in word. In my fantasy I went to a wise therapist/friend for supervision. Instead of presenting "a case," I put down my tape recorder and cried for forty-five minutes. I don't believe I shared this next reflection with her, although I am not sure, but it seemed that the reason for my tears was something about the sadness of life, the fact of death, and the inability of caring to take all the hurt away. I do remember that she asked me about my friend, and I told her briefly about how at several specific points in my life he had helped me.

After a period of silence Joanne said, "You know, I'm thinking about those clouds in the dream. I feel like looking up at them and saying, 'Come on, you muthas, let's have at it.' " I cried openly, and Joanne smiled. The session ended with Joanne coming over, hugging me, and hoping I would feel better.

The pastoral counselor is experienced as a "father, lover, and religious person." What he is seems to vary according to the needs of the counselee. In whatever he is, his humanity is very evident. Pain is experienced, and tears are shed. The relationship is more evident than anything that is said. Pastoral counseling is, however, a verbal interaction, and what is said is important. Something of the nature of that dialogue can be seen in the next clinical incident.[17]

Sam called for an appointment for his wife, Sally. She had been referred to me by a United Methodist pastor in the community who said that she needed help with her depression. Sam and Sally were newcomers to the Atlanta area, having recently moved there from a smaller city in south Georgia. Although the problem was presented as Sally's alone, I followed my custom with married persons and insisted that both of them come to the first interview.

My initial meeting with Sam and Sally, who were in their early thirties, revealed that they both had some present unhappiness and were carrying some painful baggage from the past. Sally's depression, however, seemed to be related to her lack of an interpersonal network of support in the new community where she lived and to her denial of need for such support. This resulted in Sally's placing too much of her need on Sam. Her anger, frustration, and depression resulted when Sam, though he tried could not adequately respond. Both Sam and Sally had been married before and were, therefore, overconcerned in proving that this marriage would work. They were unaware of the extent of their dependency on each other and, like most people who enter counseling for the first time, they were unaware of the depth of the human need to be parented and cared for. They felt they had to be ill or have an accident before they could ask for the help they needed.

Sally, particularly, had had some unsatisfactory parenting. Her physician father was hard-driving, a heavy drinker, and often unavailable. Her mother fought unsuccessfully to get enough personally from the marriage and also had been unavailable to Sally because of psychological or physical illness. Sally learned to take care of herself and to find enough parenting from members of her extended family to get by. An early marriage due to pregnancy and a subsequent divorce put her more on her own. She proved herself by graduating from

33

college and getting a master's degree while taking care of her child. When she hurt, she learned not to show it. What she showed was the tough southern lady who smiled graciously and took everything in her stride.

Though the major attention in the counseling was given to Sally, I continued to see the couple together. My concern, as it is more often than not, was to provide some temporary parenting, to get with the pain behind Sally's depression, and to interpret the depression, by calling it that, as normal human unhappiness related to a particular stress situation. I attempted to deal with the marriage relationship by helping Sam and Sally see what it could and could not do in satisfying individual needs and to encourage them to develop a new network of friendship and support in church and community.

During the early months of counseling, Sally became more forthright in her expression of anger, not hiding what she felt, but attempting to deal with it directly. Her depression lifted, and she and Sam worked on getting this new expression of intense feeling into their relationship. Sally began to get more in touch with her past, with its pain and deprivation, in spite of the fact that she came from an upper-class family. One afternoon Sally came in alone. Sam was out of town. She said she was depressed again, just like last fall. "I'm not able to cope," she said. "Sam can't help. Nothing's any better."

Pastoral
Counselor: What do you think is going on? Has anything in particular happened?

Sally: Well, my aunt died, but that was last week. That couldn't be it. I just can't seem to get down to work. It's just like before.

P.C.: *(Not remembering having heard much about the aunt)* Tell me more about your aunt.

Sally: *(Sally talks at length about her aunt and the way Sally's father made fun of her and didn't take her seriously.)* But she was always doing something for somebody else. I didn't really see her that often. I don't think that that's bothering me. I really should be over it.

P.C. Sally, how much do you know about grief? *(P.C. gives a mini-lecture on grief work and suggests that Aunt Rebecca may be more important to Sally than she is aware of. P. C. encourages her to tell him more about Aunt Rebecca.)*

Sally: It's so unfair. She was killed taking a blind woman across the street. *(Gives details of the accident.)*

P.C.: You sound angry.

Sally: I am. I don't see how if there is a God, he could allow this kind of thing to happen. I don't know what I believe anymore. Do you think I should talk to Jim (the pastor who had referred her)?

P.C.: It depends on whether you feel he could tolerate your doubts. Why don't you stay with it here for awhile.

Sally: *(Talks about what a bad world this is and asks why things like this happen. She gets further into her anger and wonders if her husband can tolerate it.)* Why bother living, why work, why do anything?

P.C.: It's interesting how important your aunt is to you, and that in all our months together I hardly knew anything about her.

Sally: She was there when I needed her. Whenever my mother wasn't there, it seemed like Aunt Rebecca was. *(Details several incidents)*

P.C. It sounds like she helped make you who you are.

Sally: *(Seeming to ignore the last comment)* You know, I went through her house after she died. I wanted something of hers. I took some of her violets. *(She smiles)* Aunt Rebecca could never get them to bloom.

P.C.: I suspect you have more of hers than you are aware of.

Sally: *(Again smiling)* Aunt Rebecca and I are the only ones who know how to make my grandmother's caramel cake.

P.C.: Another way you are like her. I hope you'll give me a piece of that cake sometime.

Sally: I will. *(Reflectively)* Before I went to the funeral, I was in her house, and she made a cake like that—just the day before she died. I ate three pieces of it. It was so good, I could hardly get enough. *(Silence)*

> **P.C.:** I imagine you know a bit more now about what Holy Communion means.
>
> **Sally:** *(Cries softly for awhile and then smiles)*
>
> **P.C.:** Thank you for letting me know her.

Themes from both of these cases are interpreted later. I have presented them here as examples of the type of ministry which, because they are full of meaning for me, I must bring into dialogue with the Christian story. They contribute to my understanding of relational humanness and the way I use that understanding in my interpretation of who the Christ was and is.

In this chapter I have attempted to suggest how a norm for pastoral counseling seems to have emerged from the life of the pastoral counseling movement. It is not a Procrustean, but a dialogical norm—one which can interpret and correct, but which can also be modified and enriched through active dialogue. I have also presented a theological interpretation of the Christian story, focusing on what seems to be the central elements that must be taken into account in a ministry that is related to that story. I have used some of the conclusions, if not the method, of Karl Barth to suggest how our humanity may be related to that of the Christ. And, finally, I have presented some case material important in my practice of ministry. Although the specific elements that I presented may not be the same ones that would be chosen by the reader, I am convinced that they are the type of elements, both in Christian theology and in the practice of ministry, that must be brought together if counseling is to be understood as a ministry of the Christian church.

I turn now to the ongoing dialogue that sustains the pastoral counselor in offering relational humanness—the dialogue with the role and function of the minister.

Chapter Two

The Visible Pastor—Role and Identity
in Pastoral Counseling

The pastor's ability to offer humanness in relationship is sustained by his or her ongoing dialogue with the role and function of minister and by the sense of pastoral identity that can develop as a result of participation in and reflection on that role and function. The moments like those revealed in the case material depend not only on the pastor's skill and personal availability in relationship, but also on the meaning of the ministry that he or she represents. One's ministry exists apart from how one feels about ministry at a particular point, or whether or not one is fully aware of being a minister. In pastoral counseling, for example, a counselee may find humanness in relationship through what pastoral counselors represent as well as what they are.

A significant part of what happens between Joanne and me in the case is attributed by Joanne herself to the fact that I am a "religious person." Certainly, this is not an adequate designation of what it means to be an ordained minister of the church. It does, however, underscore the importance of what the pastoral counselor represents, as well as what he or she is even for the masses of people who, though religious in some way, yet are not active participants in any community of faith. It is to this group of people that pastoral counseling so often provides ministry, and an important part of that ministry is for such persons to be with one who represents the values and commitments of Christian faith.

My long-term commitment to be a minister and my

conscious intention or lack of it to be a minister at this particular time represented the Christian community and tradition to Joanne. In his discussion of the symbolic role of the priest, Urban Holmes notes that we do not have to know "the inner intentions of the priest in order to be guaranteed the authority of his office. . . . God is present to those who engage the validly ordained priest in faith, both within the liturgy and in his extra-liturgical ministrations."[1]

Without getting into a discussion of the varying views of different Christian traditions regarding the representational function of the minister, I am emphasizing the importance of the minister's being seen as minister and the power of this fact in itself to stir up important issues both for the pastoral counselor and the counselee. One could argue about whether or not Joanne engaged me in the counseling relationship "in faith." My assumption is that her coming to me "to try to make sense of some things" was indeed a faithful act. For myself, and I believe, to some degree for all ministers, the fact that a person comes expecting something significant from that essentially inseparable mix of me and what I represent stirs a powerful dynamic within me. My inner experience tells me that I am at the same time minister and one who does not feel like a minister. I rejoice in and curse the fact that someone sees and uses me in that way. In a particular situation I may wonder whether ministry is possible and whether or not it is possible for me to be a minister. I wonder what it is and whether I can be it or do it.

At a recent annual meeting of the American Association of Pastoral Counselors, I overheard several of the registrants discussing the conference program. During the conversation about a scheduled presentation on a topic similar to that of this chapter, one of them complained, "Are we still talking about that?" The implication of the registrant's question was that this was an old issue settled long ago and irrelevant to his practice of pastoral counseling. The point of view of this chapter, in contrast, is that the issue of the minister's role and function is never finally settled either for the pastoral counseling specialist or for the parish minister, and, as suggested earlier, the fact of specialization in ministry raises the question of the nature of ministry itself.

The day before I wrote this paragraph I was consulted by two ministers of different denominations concerning this question. Both had had success and failure in ministry careers of ten to fifteen years. Both had had tension with their wives about their calling. Both had doubted the possibility of ministry among people such as those whom they had served, and yet both felt committed to do ministry and to be ministers. In the light of the hopes and ideals that each of them had brought to their careers, the answer to the question as to whether or not ministry is possible is probably no. In the light of a realistic analysis of the human situation, a chastened and accurate understanding of themselves and others, the answer is probably yes.

Part of the heritage of the pastoral care movement of the last thirty years, particularly as this is expressed in clinical pastoral education, is a methodology for dealing realistically with the question of whether ministry is possible at all and, particularly, whether it is possible *for me*. Although the original dynamic of CPE may well have been curiosity about the "new" science of psychology and the unusual world of mental patients, the element that has emerged as CPE's most distinctive feature is its concern with the identity and role of the minister. I have heard many times the complaint, "Other professions don't waste all this time worrying about their identity. Why do we bother about this?" Although I am not convinced of the accuracy of the questioner's premise, I am convinced that there is in our theological heritage as ministers a persistent concern about who we are. It is difficult for me to imagine anyone being really comfortable with a calling to carry on the work of Christ. And it is this discrepancy between one's calling to ministry and ministry actually done that is the focus of supervision in clinical pastoral education and in most of our later reflections on our ministry.

My discussion of these issues in ministry inevitably reflects the biases and limitations of my United Methodist tradition as well as my own. My contention is that these issues need to be dealt with, whatever one's tradition, if one is to be a *pastoral* counselor. Becoming minister involves both an act of the church and of the minister. Whether one is ordained or not, there is an act of confirming or commissioning one for Christian service. Like Paul, we are "made" ministers. It was done for us or given to us. Ministry is a condition created by the church through whatever process or ritual the particular faith group designates.

However, ministry is also a continuing covenant to continue what was begun at confirmation and ordination with an action and response dialogue between the minister and the church. I discuss this dialogue in some detail in chapter three. My concern here is with the minister's role, function, and identity. The point I am attempting to make is that after the initial action of the church in "making" a minister, what continues one in ministry is the way in which one is seen, the way one functions, and the way that experience in role and function contributes to one's sense of identity as a minister.

Pastoral Role

A role is an external perception of what one is and how one functions in relation to a particular society or community. It is, according to Talcott Parsons, "where personalities and social systems interpenetrate." A role is "the organized system of participation of an individual in a social system."[2] It "is the way in which the individual in his ordinary work situations presents himself and his activity to others, the ways in which he guides and controls the impressions they form of him, and the kinds of things he may and may not do while sustaining his performance before them."[3]

The concept of role, essentially a metaphor derived from the theater,[4] has two elements which are important for our purposes: visibility and function. The concept of visibility emphasizes the power of the role itself however actively one accepts or "plays" it. The concept of function underscores the importance of action in ministry however effective or ineffective that action may be. It is essential for a minister to be seen as minister by both church and community and to have the function of minister for those who view him/her that way.

Visibility is an issue for both generalist and specialist in pastoral counseling.[5] Those of us who have been involved in the process of clinical pastoral education have seen its presence as a significant issue from the first day a student comes to the clinical setting throughout most of the process of training. In almost every center for clinical pastoral education, the student is required to wear some identification indicating that he or she is a minister. In one of our clinical placements, Grady Memorial Hospital, Atlanta, Ga., the full-time student, wears a badge that gives his or her name, followed by the word, "Chaplain." The part-timers' badge has the student's name and the words, "Chaplain's Office." It is required that the part-time students be there, so they are not identified as chaplain. Our assumption about the badges is that they symbolize different degrees of the student's dialogue with the role of the minister. Though the student may tell the patient that she is not really a chaplain, but just Mary Martin, we insist that Mary Martin has no "license" to be in the hospital except as a representative of the Christian ministry and that she must have visibility as such. At least thirty years of literature in the CPE movement has insisted that this identification and dialogue with the role of the minister is a central training issue.[6] The visibility of the ministry role and the personal struggle it produced is significant in every stage and context for ministry.

This is as true for the minister who readily accepts a role-identifying symbol, such as clerical garb, as it is for the student uncomfortable in the chaplain's badge. Clerical garb may be saying openly, "I accept the fact that I am minister and am proud of that fact." What it doesn't say as openly is that no one can comfortably accept all the expectations, hopes, and anger that ministerial identity may bring with it. Other peoples' perceptions and assumptions inevitably bring the "visible minister" to the point of saying openly to himself or herself, "But I'm not that kind of minister." It's embarrassing to be thought of as "that kind of minister." In being seen as ministers we are identified with all the distortions and pettiness of church and ministry as well as with their greatness. The inner dialogue which takes place as a result of perceptions of us as ministers is also a significant part of professional identity formation, which is discussed later.

My concern here is with the mix of shame and satisfaction that is a part of the whole psychological experience of "being seen." Etymologically, *shame* has been associated with sham, "a fraudulent trick, hence an imposture: it causes sham.["] Developmentally, the roots of our struggle about being seen in a particular way are in what Erik Erikson has identified as a second developmental stage that focuses on the conflict between autonomy and shame and doubt.[8] As I become an autonomous person, I become visible. I become differentiated from family or group. I am noticed and rewarded or shamed for what I do well and for what I do not do well.

This is an extremely powerful experience which continues in some form throughout our lives. I would like the praise that comes from being positively seen, but I question whether or not it is worth the risk of not being approved and experiencing shame. It is the fundamental human experience underlying our struggle with being visible in any role. Certainly, that struggle is a major element in being a minister, and, in keeping with its rootage in our early developmental life. It is a given for life and ministry, continually to be dealt with, never escaped.[9]

Theologically, the necessity of the minister's visibility is a part of the continuing question of where the authentic Christian community really is and where genuine ministry is going on. One of the traditional ways of discussing this has been in terms of the visible and invisible church.[10] Paul Tillich's discussion of the "Spiritual Community" seem to me to move the discussion beyond that distinction. The "Spiritual Community" is "the inner *telos* of the churches" and, as such "is the source of everything which makes them churches. Both the churches and other groups may express the Spiritual Community." "The churches represent the Spiritual Community in a manifest religious self-expression, whereas the others represent the Spiritual Community in secular latency."[11]

The major difference between the "Spiritual Community" organized as a church and expressed in another group is that an essential characteristic of the church is a self-critical principle usually associated with prophetism and reformation. The church, in effect, witnesses to the fact that "Spiritual Community" is possible and critically judges itself and other groups in the light of its consciousness of that spiritual reality. The implication of Tillich's discussion of "Spiritual Community"[12] is that the church manifests a conscious witness to the possibility of Christian community and sometimes expresses it.[13] Its Protestant principle prevents the church from claiming to control or contain the "Spiritual Community." In a fragmentary or partial way it represents a norm for what community should be in the light of the new being in Jesus as the Christ.

The witnessing and representative function performed by the churches is also performed by the minister. He or she represents the possibility of transparency to the divine depth of being. Transparency is not a possession of the minister. It is, rather, a function for others of those who have received healing and revelation from the "Spiritual Community" and who have committed themselves to be consciously critical of the way in which the Christian message is mediated to others through them. In Tillich's thought there is no exclusivity or special power claim appropriate for church and ministry. What is expected of ministers is a conscious and increasing awareness of their function in ministry in relation to the norm for ministry, Jesus as the Christ.[14]

A significant part of the commitment to Christian ministry is an ongoing willingness to be identified as a minister. For Tillich one communicates the Christian gospel not by attempts to force a response to it, but as one identified with and representing the Christian message fully participating in human life and, thereby, experiencing with others the questions of life to which the Christian gospel offers the answer.[15] The presence of one identified with the Christian community makes possible consideration of a Christian interpretation of life within the conditions of human existence, not something brought in from outside. Whether one holds that ordination involves the conferring of a special gift or simply special function, it is clear that it provides for increased visibility for the person so designated and for the active performance of specific functions assigned to ordained persons by the various Christian traditions.

Pastoral Function

As a United Methodist minister, I was ordained to a ministry of "Word, Sacrament, and Order." The first two functions are fairly easy to identify with specific actions, usually preaching, or teaching, and administrating the sacraments. Order is a more diffuse concept, but it can be functionally identified with the concept of visibility in ministry. The minister witnesses to the necessity of there being appropriate form and structure in the life of the Christian community and identifies with the particular structure of his or her communion as a valid expression of this. A ministry of Order is one's expression of accountability to his/her particular communion's way of being and doing. It may involve affirmation of and identity with its confession of faith and the way of practicing it, thus acknowledging that the faith must have concrete expression if church and ministry are to exist.

Whereas the ministry of Order may involve the performance of many different functions that represent and embody one's tradition, the ministry of Word and Sacrament are related to particular functions: interpreting the meaning of the Christian message today and presenting the gospel in sacramental ways that transcend words. To continue in ordained ministry in most Christian traditions the minister must perform these functions for which he was set apart by the church. Because ordination for ministry has been so clearly identified with these functions, Christian traditions have often simply identified ordained ministry with them. Persons are understood to be ordained ministers only because they perform these functions. In my denomination, ministers in appointments "beyond the local church" are asked to report annually on their specific performance of these functions. I used to rebel at what seemed to me to be the bureaucracy's limited understanding of ministry and its identification of Christian ministry with these particular acts. I now believe that there is an important rationale for the emphasis on performing these traditional functions.

Ministers of the Word are committed to the challenge of publicly interpreting the Word, and they must do this enough so they will remain familiar with relating the gospel in an intelligible way to human life as it really is. If they do not do this they can lose touch with both the Christian message and the way it relates to life. A minister of Sacrament is committed to celebrating the sacraments in their familiar form in order to recognize and celebrate the sacramental in all of life, including the area of his or her specialized ministry. The dialogue with Sally in the previous chapter is an example of this. What studies of ritual state more generally is true of the ministry of Word and Sacrament. "Ritual serves as a paradigm for all significant action. . . . The performance of ritual . . . teaches one not only how to conduct the ritual itself, but how to conduct oneself outside the ritual space."[16]

For the ordained minister who, like the pastoral counseling specialist, spends the majority of his or her time in one aspect of ministry, the implication of this seems clear. Pastoral counseling, or whatever one's specialty function is, must be in some way continuous with and expressive of the ministry of Word and Sacrament. These functions do not have to be performed literally as a part of the counseling hour—although they may be—but they must continue to influence the way the minister conducts himself/herself "outside the ritual space." What the pastoral counselor says or does in the counseling hour should be significantly influenced by the fact that his or her vocation is preaching the gospel and celebrating the Christ event sacramentally. Wherever pastoral counseling is performed, the minister represents the fact that Word and Sacrament are present and available in a continuing way, not just at the ritual times of worship.

Paul Tillich's theology is again useful in underscoring this point. For Tillich, "transparency to the divine" is a normative concept which describes persons under the impact of the Spirit. It is an extention of his view of Jesus as the Christ being fully human but at the same time transparent to the divine "ground of being." What is true for Jesus as the Christ (and this phrase in effect means, who functioned as the Christ) is true to a lesser degree for every participant in the "Spiritual Community." Such persons exercise all the functions of a priest. They are saints by function who minister to others both within and outside the church, performing miracles as an expression of their spiritual power.

What is important here is not Tillich's terminology but his emphasis on function of ministry. Ministers are visible not only for visibility's sake, but also for mediating transparency. Even "Jesus is not good in himself, as the saints are not good in themselves." "The real meaning of sainthood," says Tillich, "is radiation, transparency to the holy—or translucency to the holy, if you prefer that word. 'Radiation' is perhaps the best, since a saint radiates the presence of the divine in a special way."[17]

Being a minister involves accepting the possibility that someone may experience the divine presence through me. My human problem, however, is that I want to control and dispense what people get from me (in actuality it is what they get *through* me, but it feels like *from* me), whereas this is not possible for me or for the church that I represent. As Tillich puts it, "Human spirit is unable to compel the divine Spirit to enter human spirit."[18] Transparency to the divine is not something which can be produced by the minister's will or skill.

Thus far I have discussed pastoral function in terms of the minister's whole person as it may reveal divine depth to another and in doing so bring healing. Because an acceptance of the Protestant principle, as Tillich defines it, prevents us from identifying any one action, even the administration of the sacraments, as always ministry, one is tempted to separate action from theological thinking about ministry and be satisfied with an understanding of ministry that deals only with who and what the minister is. What follows from this is an assumption that ministers function for others only through their being and that what they do is automatically ministry or that their action does not affect who they are. Both views are held more often by the question being avoided than by either view being actively espoused.

My view is that what the minister is and what he or she does are essential to an adequate concept of ministry. Commitment *to* and function in ministry require both a willingness to *be* something, to *do* something, and to *reflect* on how being and doing are related within a person. I have made explicit use of some of Tillich's theology, but my basic position is not dependent on concepts from within that system of thought. Tillich's understanding of transparency is simply a useful example of one pole of an adequate ministry theory—the representative, given, and unmanipulatable. The other necessary pole is some understanding of appropriate action for others. Ministry takes place through the actual risk of that which is represented—the divine or holy—through professional technical, and manageable skills.

With respect to the question of how technical or practical knowledge is acquired and integrated into the practice of ministry, the modern pastoral care tradition has something significant to contribute. Books by the score continue to be written on how to do various types of ministry. With respect to pastoral care, many are what Seward Hiltner calls the "hints and helps" books.[19] The question of how these techniques are ministry is generally not dealt with except through the assumption that the author's identity, or experience in ministry, makes them so. I do not mean to be unnecessarily critical of this type of material. All of us who have taught at any level in the so-called "practical" fields of ministry have taught techniques, probably, in most cases, to the benefit of our students.

Other hints on what to do come out of the secular fields. A number of years ago Carl Rogers wrote a very influential article entitled, "The Characteristics of a Helping Relationship."[20] It is still an interesting and useful contribution to a person's thinking about what it means to help. From that article, however, a mass of literature has developed which purports to train persons in achieving the characteristics which Rogers described.[21] As valuable as some of this literature can be in understanding the counseling process and in providing practice in the development of technical skills, it is peripheral to the development of the pastoral counselor.

The supervisory model[22] developed in clinical pastoral education is the central feature in facilitating the formation of a *pastoral* counselor. For students this means: (1) *involvement,* experiencing a situation that calls for ministry in which their ministry is actually needed (clinical settings need to be adequate educationally so that the student is actually needed); (2) *action,* doing something in spite of the fact that they are not thoroughly trained beforehand in what should be done; and (3) *reflection,* examining what was done in that particular context with respect to its appropriateness to the setting and to the student's own emerging style of ministry.

The genius of learning in this way has been CPE's attempt to be true both to the context of ministry and to the particular ministry of the student. It is like other skill training in that it focuses on what the student does, but it is significantly different because its major concern is not simply that a skill be learned but that a particular style of action be understood and developed by the student. This emphasis on the student's emerging style is the practical impetus for CPE's attempt to bring action into dynamic relation with being—what one is and what one does, each contributing to the enrichment of the other.

Pastoral Identity

The acquisition of the practical knowledge of ministry, particularly the ministry of pastoral care and counseling cannot be adequately discussed without examination of the concept of pastoral identity. How a minister is seen and what he does in ministry contribute significantly to the sense of *being* a pastor. Although statements about the identity of a pastor reach far back into the Christian tradition, Erik Erikson's concept of ego identity has enriched the meaning of that strand of the tradition. For Erikson, ego identity is a statement about the past, the present, and the future.

> A sense of "ego identity" emerges; it is an "accrued confidence" that starts from the very first moment of life but in the second or third decades reaches a point of decisive substance, or indeed fails to do so. Confidence about what? Confidence that somehow in the midst of change one *is*; that is one has an inner sameness and continuity which others can recognize and which is so certain that it can unselfconsciously be taken for granted. The emphasis is on what has taken place that enables what is to continue to be.[23]

Identity, according to Hans Frei, who defines the concept generically in order to discuss the identity of Jesus Christ, is

> the very "core" of a person toward which everything else is ordered. . . . It is something which, if one knows it, provides the "clue" to a person. Identity is the specific uniqueness of a person, what really counts about him, quite apart from both comparison and contrast to others.[24]

Pastoral identity involves the confidence that in the midst of changing circumstances I *am* a pastor and that in many ways I can take this for granted. To myself I *feel* like a pastor and, therefore, do not have to be concerned about this when I attempt to offer ministry to another person. Because pastoral identity is only a part of my total identity and is one of the later developing parts, it is more vulnerable to identity diffusion as a result of changes in role and function. With respect to this professional identity there is a more delicate balance among my role, function, and identity than there is with respect to my total ego identity. The professional identity is not as solidly formed because it is a later developing part of my identity and because it makes up only a portion of who I am. In fact, it may sometimes be competitive with older dimensions of my ego identity.

This means, I believe, that for my pastoral identity to have the "accrued confidence" that Erikson sees as forming one's ego identity, there must be a continual re-inforcement of role, function, and identity. I am a pastor because I have been recognized by the church as having sufficient "gifts and graces" to be ordained to a particular ministry. I am a pastor, further, because I am seen as a pastor. I function as one, and I experience myself as one. I may function as a pastor without experiencing myself as such, or I may be seen that way and understood that way without feeling that way myself. Pastoral role and function may exist without pastoral identity, but pastoral identity cannot continue without participation in pastoral role and function. In order to continue to *be* a pastor in any meaningful way—and this includes having a pastoral identity—one must be seen as minister, act as one, and reflect on the meaning of both.[25]

But how is one's pastoral identity related to what the Christ was and is?

Bernard Cooke, in his massive study of the Christian ministry, comments:

> All Christian ministry finds its origin in the salvific ministry of Jesus Himself; throughout history, Christian theology is united in recognizing this principle. There has also been agreement on the principle that all authentic Christian ministry involves a participation in Christ's ministerial mission and power, but there has been considerable disagreement as to the nature of this participation.[26]

With respect to the form of a Christian pastoral identity, Tillich is again helpful in addressing the problem of what participation in Christ's ministry means. He holds that every human being is asked to "take on the form of the Christ." This, however, can never mean copying concrete traits of his personality from what we can discern in the biblical picture. Rather, the specific characteristics of Jesus point beyond their contingent character to the new being. Jesus "is the bearer of the New Being in the totality of his being, not in any special expression of it."[27] Tillich's Christology attempts to avoid the problem of either interpreting Christ's person (Incarnation) in terms of his work (Atonement) or his work in terms of his person.

The form of Christ is his unity with God and the unity within himself. What he is and does are not separated. A clear implication of this view is that there is a dialectical relationship between Christ's person and work which continually informs and enriches each other. Frei's view of identity amplifies this meaning in a useful way. A person's specific deeds are the focus of his or her identity. Identity is also a person's manifestation as a total being ". . . the continuity of the person as he persists through all the changes that take place in his life." The identity of Jesus is in "his *intention-action* description. His specific identity was what he did and underwent." It may also be seen in his continuity through "transitions brought about by his acts and life's events . . . a certain elusive and unfinished, but also persistent, quality."[28]

Both Tillich and Frei describe a unity of Christ's person and work as constitutive of who he was—his identity. In contrast with this, all other persons do not express fully who they are by what they do. Action and being are separated. The form of Christ therefore, is "taken" as a quest, not an accomplishment. "Taking the form of Christ" can be usefully understood as a quest for unity between one's action and one's being in the process of offering ministry to others.

The form of the Christ that the Christian minister takes, whatever the specific expressions of that form in particular situations, is a never completed quest for unity. "Under the conditions of existence," as Tillich puts it, this unity can only be achieved in a fragmentary and temporary way. The term implies a continuing search for a difficult, if not impossible, goal and an attitude toward one's action that gives purpose and satisfaction to events in life which might otherwise seem unrelated and meaningless. The quest is a conscious venture of the minster. It is, therefore, an experience that is available for personal reflection and pastoral supervision.

What I have been arguing is that a major part of what makes one a minister is the way one is seen, the way one functions, and the way one reflects on that function. I am certainly not attempting to deny the "givenness" of being a minister, the necessity of the church's setting one apart for a particular task. My concern, however, has been with the minister's response to this givenness of ministry—his or her side of the dialogue with the Christ and the church. The response of the minister to being set apart for service is a willingness to be visible in spite of the inevitable ambiguity of that action and to reflect on both what one is and does. All three dimensions of this response are a part of the quest for unity between one's action and being in ministry, a way of understanding what it means to "take the form of Christ" or to participate "in Christ's ministerial mission and power."

One of my favorite illustrations of the struggle involved in achieving a genuinely human pastoral identity comes from a clinical pastoral education group that I supervised many years ago. It was previously published in a *festshrift* dedicated to Seward Hiltner,[29] but variations on this same theme continue to emerge among both beginning theological students and experienced pastors. The human condition continues to challenge us, in whatever context we may experience it.

In this particular incident, one of the students began the session by reading a selection from Calvin as a devotional. After a few moments of silence, another student responded with a question which had apparently been stirred by his experiences of functioning as and reflecting on being a minister:

> **Doug:** What does the reading you just read from Calvin mean? Let me see (the book), can I? I mean—I've heard crap

like that all my life, and I have never been able to figure what they are talking about. *(There is a pause while Doug finds the place, and then he begins to read from the Calvin passage.)* "Let this be the first step—abandon ourselves and devote the whole energy of our mind to the service of God." Abandoning yourself—what does that mean? I mean it seems to me in these weeks I'm learning to understand myself and to know myself, and a lot of things I am finding out aren't pretty, but I am learning how to express my feeling. I'm trying to get over my reluctance to show my anger, and these are the kinds of things I hear Calvin saying are bad—are sinful.

The first response of the group to Doug's quest for unity between the ideas he had heard all his life and his new awareness of his feelings was an attempt to reinterpret the ideas involved in the passage from Calvin. Bob, the student who had read the passage, responded to Doug's feelings by ignoring them and the struggle they represented. He used his intellectual ability to interpret the material read in its larger context and to discuss a similar idea as it appears in Thomas á Kempis' *Of the Imitation of Christ*. Then a member of the group, who was more practically, than historically oriented spoke up.

Bill:	What was that book that made such a big hit along the same line?
Supervisor:	*In His Steps?*
Bill:	I was real impressed with that to begin with, but then I began to start thinking about acting as Christ would act in every situation that I found, and that's a hell of a way to live. *(Pause)*
Joe:	What's the difference, sandals?
Bill:	I just don't think that we are called to imitate anybody. I'm trying to find out who I am, you know, this business. I want to be me, and me may not be like Jesus.
Doug:	How would you preach a sermon on "Let this mind be in you which is in Christ Jesus," the *kenosis* passage?
Bill:	I've never preached on that.

Up this this point in the discussion I had stayed in the background waiting to see whether what appeared to me to be Doug's quest for some kind of integration or unity would be ignored or picked up by the members of the group. Bill did move in quickly to express his feelings of frustration and failure in attempting an imitative taking of the form of Christ. What Tillich calls a way of barren legalism in which acts once imitated lose their power to point beyond themselves, Bill emotionally referred to as "a hell of a way to live." Joe, flippantly but with some of his own conflict showing, suggested that it would be simpler if the conflict could be resolved by putting on something external like sandals. Bill responded by characterizing the predicament of the Christian minister, "Me may not be like Jesus." Doug refocused the question by bringing a biblical statement of the same problem, and Bill gave up the struggle of dealing with the question, at least for awhile, by saying, "I've never preached on that."

Without the structured opportunity to reflect on his ministry, Bill would probably have moved onto the next situation calling for pastoral work either ignoring the value of his past experience or carrying with him the anger or guilt about having been neither like Jesus nor like himself.

Fortunately, Joe has not let his quip about the sandals rest with its cleverness but continues to feel the conflict and begins to relate it to his actual experience of ministry in the hospital. Here for the first time in his life he has found situations for which he does not have appropriate words or actions.

> **Joe:** A guy who really gets involved with people has got to risk getting hurt. You know a boxer who gets in the ring can't be too proud of his nose. I've always been proud of mine.
>
> **Supervisor:** Maybe that's what *kenosis* means for you—giving up pride in your nose.
>
> **Joe:** Getting it busted!
>
> **Supervisor:** Maybe so.

Joe: One of the feelings I have here in the hospital is that I would be a whole lot better off if I were completely armor-plated or didn't have to wear any armor at all. This business of being somewhere in the middle—allowing for yourself and your own reactions—

Joe, in contrast to Bill, stays with the tension he is experiencing between his action and being. The broken nose is a symbol of the kind of total involvement of himself with others that because of Joe's skill with words has not thus far been necessary in ministry. The tension or conflict in his being a minister is symbolized further by the fact that he is always "somewhere in the middle." Ministers must wear their role and express themselves through it even though they often wish they were free of the tradition they represent. The becoming minister feels awkward in the inherited "armor" of his profession, and in him is something of the young David who wishes to junk it all and choose his own five smooth stones. But to continue with our illustration:

Joe: Aren't there some ways around this dilemma?
Doug: Lead with your nose.
Joe: Right! *(Talking excitedly to me)* And like you said two sessions ago, you have to go back to Mr. Walters' room for him to die. *(Joe is referring to the fact that I had insisted that he return to visit a dying patient in spite of the fact that he felt very anxious and could think of nothing to say.)* I tell you before then the possibility had never occurred to me—in other situations in my life to go back when I was going to fail.

Doug tells Joe that the way to deal with the tension he is experiencing is further involvement and risk, not an abstract search for answers. Go *be* with Mr. Walters when you have nothing to say in the face of his death, and some of the tension between action and being, between the person and the role, will be resolved.

I had underscored this point with a symbol used earlier in

the session and indicated that the kind of "emptying" or giving up pride in one's nose, or in Tillich's terms, claiming ultimacy for any aspect of one's finite nature, is a process, not an accomplishment.

Supervisor I sounds like more *kenosis* to me.
Joe: It's taken awhile for this to get to be an option.
Supervisor: It may take awhile longer too.
Doug: This kind of emptying I like! It's genuine, it's real. Now maybe there's a level that you can get to after you've led with your nose for awhile—been pounded. This other type of self-denial, I just feel like I'm wrapped in cords—bound—and I'm experiencing from that—I mean I'm experiencing freedom coming from Joe. This is a type of emptying I like.

It is characteristic of clinical illustrations that they never fully exemplify what is being stated more theoretically. This one, however, seems to me to come closer than most. It points to the minister's quest for a unity of who he or she is with what is done in ministry, some of the risk involved in seeking it, and one way of conceptualizing how this may be related to the self-giving ministry of Christ for us. If the quest for unity is indeed a never-ending one, then the concept is relevant for a minister at mid-career as well as for students in CPE. It is the nature of ministry for the minister to be concerned about whether or not it is possible *for me* to be a minister.

The question of whether or not ministry is possible grows out of the nature of the human situation. Human brokenness is resistive to all the technologies of human helping. In fact, part of my own brokenness is that I tend to distort my view of life so that it is separated into problems that I can or cannot solve. I easily fool myself into thinking that all I have to do is to find the right combination of words and actions or secure the services of another person who does have the right combination. I seem to have to learn over and over that that's not the way it is. There is no such thing as pastoral cure, only pastoral care, and part of my condition is to doubt whether that can be enough. Like Joe I have trouble going back to Mr. Walters' room to watch him die. I have no argument other than that of my own experience and the experience of others I have known, but it seems to me to be part of what it means to be a minister to doubt whether or not ministry is possible and, even more clearly, to doubt whether ministry is possible for me.

In the following chapter this question is examined in relation to the Christian community which identifies me as a minister. The struggle of which I speak here is not with the church and my embarrassment with it, but with myself. I have spent a good deal of time and money trying to identify what is realistic for me to do and be as a minister. I recall both the pain and triumph when I first said no to a valued church member. It was a moment of self-assertion and freedom, but also one in which I began to realize that no matter how much I learned, there was no way in which I could respond adequately to all the human hunger to which I would be exposed, whether it was realistic or not. Moreover I began to suspect that my sensitivity to the relational hunger of others had something to do with my own. I recalled the words of one of the most perceptive human beings I have known, John Warkentin, a psychotherapist in Atlanta, who once said to me, "I believe that to do what you propose to do with your life, you will have to become a patient." It took me several years to realize the accuracy of that observation. A church school superintendent, who was convinced that the Lord was telling him to do the opposite of what the official decision of the church had been, helped stir my rage enough to decide that perhaps he was not the only one who was "crazy." Several years later it became clear to me that although I thought psychotherapy was a good thing, I would never have enough of it—or perhaps anything else—to enable me to be the kind of minister I wanted to be. I hoped that my student, Doug, was right. Perhaps there is a level of being a minister "that you can get to after you've led with your nose for awhile—been pounded," but I was convinced that I had not yet made it. Nor did I know anyone whom I thought had.

Chapter Three

A Not-So-Private Practice—Accountability in Pastoral Counseling

The third ongoing dialogue which sustains the minister in offering pastoral counseling is the dialogue with the communities that correct and confirm his or her ministry. In discussing the minister's role and identity in chapter 2, I suggested that being a minister is both a condition and a continuing covenant. In this chapter I present some of the ways in which both minister and community can be faithful to that covenant, and I also describe some of the issues that should be involved in the dialogue between them. Most of the structures of accountability for ministry are related to parish work; therefore, pastoral counseling, which is not usually a part of the regular ministry to the parish, needs new structures for facilitating the relationship of pastoral counseling to the church.

In 1959, Gibson Winter, then an assistant professor of Ethics and Society at the University of Chicago, published an article in *Pastoral Psychology* entitled, "The Pastoral Counselor Within the Community of Faith." Although the details of that article are not important after more than twenty years, Winter's closing comments are. "Because the pastor represents Christ's fellowship in his counseling, we can see in this process a microcosmic concentration of the broader action of the Christian community. As this representation is understood and made a reality in the Christian community, the ministry of pastoral counseling can upbuild Christian fellowship instead of becoming a substitute for it."[1] Winter's was one of the early voices insisting that the pastoral counselor remain a part of the community of faith and that the counseling relationship not be seen as a substitute for Christian fellowship. I would like to reaffirm both of those concerns, but reinterpret their meaning in the light of the present situation and the development of pastoral counseling during the last twenty years.

At this point pastoral counseling, whether offered by a parish minister or a pastoral counseling specialist, is fundamentally a ministry of the church to those outside its life. My concern is not to analyze the factors in society and in the church that have contributed to this, but to affirm the appropriateness of the image of the sheep separated from the flock as an accurate one for describing most of those who come for pastoral counseling. Whether it takes place in a pastoral counseling center or in the privacy of the pastor's office in the parish, pastoral counseling today is usually separated from other functions of the church. The pastoral counselor, whether parish minister or counseling specialist, is ministering to the same persons whom the evangelist would want to reach. Pastoral counseling, however, has less direct "pay-off" for the parish than evangelism because most of those who are ministered to outside the "fold" do not choose to come in, or, at least, not to that particular congregation. Like the evangelist, the pastoral counselor may have difficulty maintaining adequate structures of accountability for his work with persons presently estranged from the church.

The comparison between pastoral counseling and evangelism is not one that reveals similarity at all points, nevertheless it does illuminate some features of pastoral counseling and the pastoral counselor that have not been sufficiently discussed. Although the relationship of the pastoral counselor to the church may be a relatively new issue, the relationship of the evangelist to the church is not. Church history is filled with problems of those who, in reaching out to those estranged from the community themselves became similarly estranged. The problem as expressed in the last twenty years with it is a problem not only for the pastoral counseling specialist but for the parish minister as well. Ministers who "spend too much time in counseling" almost always will develop some significant tension with the laity of their churches and with the judicatory officials who support their work.

Most of the pastoral counseling of members of the community of faith is not done by the pastor of that community except when the "problem" as perceived by the parishioner is understood to be external to his or her person. Although the parish church continues to ritualize and symbolize the forgiveness of sin for its members, it is less likely to be a resource for exploring what that sin means in the life of a particular person. Thus, it is more accurate to say that most pastoral counseling takes place *in relation to* the community of faith or is representative of it, rather than *within it*.

It may be that the parish church and its pastor *should* offer the kind of community where such issues can effectively be explored, but many—I believe the majority of persons at this particular time do not seem to perceive it that way. They may be an active part of a particular parish, hearing the Word, receiving the Sacrament, and participating in the fellowship, but the majority of them do not understand their particular church and pastor as offering a place where sin can be explored as well as forgiven. (I do not have statistical documentation of the above contention. I believe it to be factual on the basis of hundreds of reports by counselees of my own and my colleagues who state that they have come to a pastoral counseling center because of this feeling.) The church is perceived by many as being like the story of the revival meeting where the preacher keeps encouraging the convicted brother to confess one sin after another and to, "Tell it all, brother." When he finally confesses the last and worst sin the preacher says, "If I'd been you, I wouldn't have confessed that."

The story is a caricature, but is not inaccurate to the real story with many variations that I have heard again and again. A person who risks sharing a painful part of his or her life with a person or a sharing group in the church and finds that while certain sins seem understood and accepted, others are rejected, will experience estrangement rather than affirmation. The parish church is a place where the issues of deepest personal meaning are dealt with, but each parishioner reserves the right to say in what way those issues will be dealt with for him or her. The pastor and laity of that congregation may be extremely important and may have been supportive and helpful to a person, but they may not be the ones to be trusted with the details of that person's particular human predicament. That church may be an important witness to the reality of the Spiritual Community, yet still not be its embodiment for many of its members at certain points in their lives.

Tillich's distinction between the church as both sociological and spiritual is helpful in interpreting the circumstance that I have been discussing. "The paradox of the churches is the fact that they participate, on the one hand, in the ambiguities of life in general and of the religious life in particular and, on the other hand, in the unambiguous life of the Spiritual Community."[2] In its sociological reality a particular church may fail to offer genuine community and acceptance to its members even when it represents to them the Christian understanding of community and enables them to recognize and experience community elsewhere.

The church's more important task is witnessing to the possiblity of Spiritual Community whether or not at a particular time it is able to provide it. This is not minimizing the importance of the church. It is, rather, an expression of the Protestant principle that prevents any one expression of community from claiming to control or contain it. The church's primary function is to represent the norm for what community should be in the light of Jesus as the Christ, even when it is unable to embody that norm in any consistent way.

After acknowledging the difficulty of parish ministers to offer a long-term ministry of pastoral counseling to persons vitally involved in their parish, it is important to affirm that many parish ministers are well qualified to offer excellent pastoral counseling. Moreover, it is valuable for pastoral work in general that parochial ministers have training in the type of counseling that acknowledges the problem to be "within me" rather than "out there." Beyond the fact that it offers one more caring person to a world in need of care, pastoral counseling sensitizes pastors to the depth of human brokenness and to the power of grace enabling one to transcend it in even limited ways. Pastoral counseling is a major contributor to reducing trivia in the Christian witness, and that is important in the light of the church's task of interpreting the Christian message.

Private Practice

Because pastoral counseling is not usually a ministry offered to members of the parish, it is essential that the work be approved and validated by an official group within the parish and by the appropriate officials beyond the local church to which the minister is accountable. Sessions, administrative boards or vestries need to know and approve if the pastor is spending the equivalent of a day a week in pastoral counseling to persons who are not related to the parish. Without this kind of accountability the minister is engaged in private practice or in a relationship that has many of the characteristics of an affair.

Private practice is the practice of any function in which the practitioner is accountable only to himself or herself and to the person to whom the service is provided. Certainly there are accountabilities to the state, to the profession, and to others affected by the practice, but *private* practice clearly means a very limited accountability. Further, the practice of whatever it is—psychotherapy, public speaking, teaching, evangelism, involves the exchange of fees for the services rendered.

The church has been and continues to be concerned both about any private practice of ministry functions and about the money received for such functions. In my experience, however, much of the concern seems to be misplaced, its underlying rationale more competitive than theological. One of the most common human fantasies is that anyone who is not subject to exactly the same restraints as I am is in some way bound to be doing better than I am. That doesn't seem fair to me—at least not to me at my most narcissistic and competitive self; therefore, something needs to be done about that person. It is true that something needs to be done, but what it is grows out of the theological principle that all ministry is integrally related to the community that authorizes it, not that all of it needs to be the same or that it shouldn't threaten my feelings of adequacy.

With respect to fees for service, in relation to the principle of accountability, the problem comes not at the point of the way that the service is paid for or the amount paid, but the secrecy about it. As one of my colleagues has often said, "I need someone to check on my greed." Unfortunately the church has not always said or done this openly, but has focused on more peripheral issues. Clergy of all types have received fees for a variety of services. Services provided for persons outside the life of the parish may both supplement the minister's income and stimulate his or her professional development and parish work. The problem with private practice as a part of ministry is its secrecy, its likeness to an affair. The problem with fee income for clergy, whether it comes from psychotherapy or the holding of evangelistic services, is the common practice of keeping that income secret from the groups to which the minister is accountable. Accountability does not mean uniformity, but open dialogue in which there is commitment to and understanding of ministry on the part of both church and minister.

Accountability for Ministerial Function

Because ministry is a visible function, sustained by a particular unit of the Christian community, it must be reported on by the minister who provides it to the appropriate authority within the church. That authority or authorities should participate with the pastor in decisions about the kind of ministry he or she is offering on their behalf and the means by which it may realistically be paid for. The minister needs support for and understanding of what he or she is doing. Critical questions should be asked about the minister's function as a pastoral counselor in relation to the life and mission of the particular congregation, presbytery, or conference. None of these questions need violate confidentiality or limit inappropriately the way in which the pastoral counseling is carried out, but what is actually being done in this part of the pastor's ministry needs to be reported to the church in something other than a *pro forma* way.

Whether a minister is in a parish, counseling center, or other setting for ministry, three important dimensions of the accountability dialogue should take place between him/her and the church. These dimensions form the structure of accountability within the relationship between church and minister. This structure may be described in terms of participation, interpretation, and confirmation.

First, in order to maintain their relationship to the church which ordained them, ministers need to be active participants in a particular Christian community in which the gospel is proclaimed, interpreted for today, and its message celebrated and experienced. For the parish pastor with major responsibilities for this type of ministry, it would seem to be obvious that participation would be taking place. It is obvious that his or her duties require what Tillich calls mediating, conveying to others what has been received. It is less obvious that what is mediated is continuing to be received. The question for all ministers, whatever their setting for ministry, is, How am I continuing to receive the Christian gospel and to participate in a community that celebrates it?

Another way to express and broaden the meaning of that question is to put it in more Pauline terms, How am I working out my own salvation with fear and trembling? How is the quest continuing for a richer and deeper understanding of the gospel message? Some of the answers to these questions may be put in terms of how often the minister has worshiped, listened to the gospel interpreted, or participated in continuing education. Part of the dialogue between minister and church should be put in these factual ways. Unfortunately, the structure for this sort of accountability has often been left at this level. The real issue is a deeper one. The minister who continues to be minister must provide opportunities for continuing participation as a communicant, student, and receiver of ministry. He or she must be open to receive from clergy and laity in some particular, fallible Christian community. One is able to continue in Christian ministry and remain accountable to the church body which ordains by participating in Christian community as a receiver of the gospel.

Second, the minister is accountable through the interpretation of his or her ministry. As with participation it seems easier to assume that the parish minister's work would automatically be interpreted as Christian ministry, whereas the minister who works outside the parish setting would have a more difficult interpretive task. The central issue for all ministers, whatever the setting in which they work, is whether or not the tasks that they undertake are sufficiently important when examined in the light of the Christian message. The answer to that question can be uncomfortable for any minister, and he or she is accountable to the church when that question is asked, explored individually, and openly interpreted and discussed with responsible officials of the community to which he or she is accountable. Although the titles of the church officials and groups who deal with this question varies from communion to communion, the issue is important in all traditions. The minister has responsibility for some public accounting of what has been done in ministry and how what has been done is related to the central concerns of the gospel.

In addition to interpreting to the church how what they do in the name of Christ is indeed Christian ministry, ordained ministers also are responsible to interpret to the community that ordains them how they are faithful to the confession or other system of belief and practice of their particular communion. How is what one does in ministry related to the theology and practice of ministry in one's own church or denomination? How is one involved in practicing the beliefs of one's particular Christian tradition? The whole concept of "sustaining dialogue" that I have used in these three chapters rejects any rigidly interpreted confessional standard. It does insist, however, that the minister take seriously the question, How is my ministry continuous with the ministry of my particular tradition? This is not a task of conformity, but one of interpretation.

For example, as a pastoral counselor I attempt to help persons break the bonds of perfectionism in their lives. At the same time, as a United Methodist minister I am obligated by the vows which I took in joining the Annual Conference to take seriously and to interpret for our time and my life what it means theologically to "go on to perfection."

"Coherently deforming" my tradition—and this obviously requires much more interpretive work than can appropriately be done here—I trust in the power of God to make me "perfect in love in this life." I do not believe that in the same way that John Wesley seemed to understand it psychologically; but as an affirmation of the incredible possibility of God's grace to impact my particular life, "I do so believe." As a statement of my possible achievement in relation to any other person, "going on to perfection"[3] seems preposterous. As a reminder of my calling as a Christian not to be satisfied with the hurt in the world, it is an important part of my traditional beliefs.

Methodist peculiarities are not germain to everyone, but in every Christian tradition there are apparent inconsistencies between theology and life. The minister's task is to take them seriously, not too quickly dismissing one side or the other, but, as I suggested in chapter 1, "coherently deforming" the tradition in order to maintain continuity with it.

Third, accountability to the church requires that responsible persons or groups within the setting where the clergyperson is offering ministry confirm that ministry is taking place. In the parish, community mental health center, or denominational structure, there must be those who offer confirmation that ministry is taking place. In the parish setting this seems to be a more or less routine part of congregational life. Often the questions need to be clarified and made more critically effective, but denominations often provide consultation and training for doing this. Outside the parish, and particularly in a secular setting, the task is more difficult. It is not the purpose of such settings to evaluate ministry as ministry. What the clergyperson does is usually interpreted in another type of language. Nevertheless, it is the responsibility of an agency that employs an ordained clergyperson to become acquainted enough with the language of the church to provide confirmation that ministry, understood in the church's terms, is taking place. The minister working there must assist in this interpretive process, but the agency or the consumer of the services offered should be able to say, in some way, that as a result of the minister's work, "the blind see, the lame walk." Where ordained ministry is taking place, the gospel story must be known well enough to make possible this kind of confirmation of the actions of ministry.

To be sure, a secular agency is only secondarily an interpreter of ministry. It is primarily a provider of services. In that kind of setting what you call it should be considerably less important than whether or not it does anybody any good. In this context, ministers offer their services along with secular providers and must demonstrate their usefulness on an open market. For ordination to Christian ministry to continue to have meaning, however, both the ministry event and a witness to the meaning of that event by the community in which it takes place are necessary.[4]

Accountability for Professional Competence

I have taken the position that in order to be a minister, one must practice ministry, not in private, but in a publicly accountable way. I have suggested a threefold accountability for ministry described in terms of participation, interpretation, and confirmation. I have not attempted to demonstrate how each of these dimensions of accountability are rooted in the Christian tradition, although I believe such a case could be made. My concern continues to be more contemporary and functional, how the parish minister and the specialist in pastoral counseling share a common process of accountability and relationship to the Christian community.

Because this accountability is primarily a public one—open at least to all members of the church—the ministry of pastoral counseling needs to have an additional accountability, a clinical accountability for one's pastoral care and counseling practice and for all dimensions of ministry which involve the deeply personal. The minister needs to talk about his relationships to persons without violating confidence and being disrespectful to the persons to whom he or she ministers. This type of accountability requires relationship to a community that is seldom built into the structure of the church.

If pastors are to be significantly related to the community of faith they must have a community in which the deepest matters of faith and doubt, sin and human brokenness may be discussed. If ministers are bound by confidentiality not to discuss these deeply personal matters of life in a way in which they can grow in their ability to deal with them, then they are separated from some of the more important experiences of Christian community. The young pastor who anxiously stumbled into our pastoral counseling center looking for an expert to tell him what to do about a church member's homosexuality needed a good deal more than that. I could take a few minutes to let him ventilate some of his panic, support some of the things he had intuitively done that were helpful, and suggest some limits as to what he could do. What he needed more than an individual consultant whom he had chanced to find was a regular place to go where he could deal with experiences in his life and work that frightened and challenged him.

The individual congregation cannot provide this for its pastor. It can accept his or her inexperience and incompetence in a general way, offering support and care. It cannot, however, deal with the specific instances in which the pastor's immaturity and sin have been revealed in the concrete reality of pastoral work or with the expected or unexpected sin of one of its members. The pastor needs a different community to which that kind of clinical accountability can be expressed. There are deeper, more important questions to be dealt with than, What can I do about homosexuals? And these questions can seldom be raised in the parish or even with the church officials beyond the parish to whom the minister is responsible. Pastors who work in depth with persons—whatever the type of pastoral relationship—need a non-parochial structure for supervision and/or consultation.

Supervision and Consultation

A number of distinctions can be made between supervision and consultation. The most common and most useful has to do with the responsibility for the ministry for which supervision or consultation is sought. In supervision, supervisors have some responsibility for the ministry being done; in consultation, they do not. In the circumstance most familiar to me, if a clinical pastoral education student is ineffective in the area of the hospital where the student is assigned, the chaplain supervisor's own ministry as well as the training program may be threatened. Both the supervisor and the student have something at stake in the provision of pastoral services in the student's area of the hospital. The degree of threat to the supervisor caused by student ineffectiveness varies from situation to situation, but without some such responsibility and resultant anxiety, a supervisory situation does not exist. In consultation, the consultant responds to the situation presented with all the knowledge and skill that he or she may have, but the person for whom the consultation is provided has all the responsibility for the situation.

The most common confusion between supervision and consultation has come from the assumption that consultation is a relationship between peers and supervision is between a more experienced or qualified person and one who is inexperienced. The intent of this distinction has been to insure that a student preparing for practice in a particular field would be required to learn from more experienced practitioners as well as from peers. Thus, a candidate doing a certain amount of work with someone trained in assisting is a requirement by professional organizations, such as the American Association of Pastoral Counselors or the American Association of Marriage and Family Therapists. My concern here is to insist that in developing one's practice of Christian ministry, both supervision, where one is involved with a more experienced minister in the same situation of ministry, and consultation, where the use of the help of another is technically optional, are essential.

In both the supervision of one's ministry and consultation about one's ministry, the primary focus of concern is what I have called "the quest for unity between one's action and being," not just how one performs a particular ministry or understands one's counselee. Both supervision and consultation most often fail when one of these dimensions is dealt with to the exclusion of the other. A focus on being alone would move too far into the psychotherapeutic realm whereas a focus only on what has been done would degenerate into simply the teaching of techniques. Pastoral supervision at its best attempts to maintain an appropriate tension between the two. For pastors who have achieved significant maturity in their personal identity and their professional self, supervision can be more centered on methodology. The person using the method, however, can never be lost sight of. One of the reasons that group supervision and consultation is so important is that a group is seldom able to be "conned" into looking only at the case and not at the person presenting it.

With even the most experienced individual supervisors, this tends to happen. They get to know their supervisee so well that they relax into technical teaching. To offer their best, individual supervisors and consultants themselves need to be accountable for their work to a group of peers in ministry.

Pastoral Counseling Supervision

An example of the necessary move from method to person as it occurs in pastoral supervision may be seen in this example of pastoral counseling supervision. The student, a minister in his late thirties, had been involved in counseling a middle-aged woman for several weeks. He reads to the supervisor from his handwritten notes about what has been happening in the counseling relationship:

Edmund: Somehow Ellen (the counselee) does get fed, although in an indirect fashion. When I try to meet her directly, especially as directly as I try to meet Bob (another counselee), this mask seems to come over her face. I don't get any feeling. I don't get any response. I just feel like she freezes into an icicle and then the result is, well, just like now. Two weeks ago she canceled last week's appointment and then she canceled again for today. I have a feeling that there is a forty-four-year-old women and perhaps, this is an occasion when perhaps I ought to try to tread a bit more softly and carefully.

Supervisor: I'm interested in hearing more about your loud treading. *(Edmund pauses and then gives an illustration out of the last session of Ellen's freezing up.)* What did you do when she did this?

Edmund: I said nothing I had the sense of "Ellen, it's your turn." Say something.

Supervisor: Is this your style when a woman freezes on you?

Edmund: It's been my style with her.

Supervisor: If it's just with her, what's different with her that causes you to let it go?

Edmund: The feeling I have when she does that is that this is more than she can take and that this is something that she has patterned over twenty-two years of marriage.

Supervisor: If you're saying this is transference from her past to your relationshp with her, is there any way you can help her see this?

Edmund It strikes me that I might say something like, I wonder if that was the way you froze with Morton (her husband) when he was drunk and screaming at you? Is this the kind of cold shoulder that you turned toward him? I'm not drunk, I'm not screaming.

Supervisor: *(Interrupts)* Stop!

Edmund: O. K. I hear you.

Supervisor: I don't think you need all of that explanation to get her attention.

Edmund: *(Laughing)* I do.

Supervisor: *(Laughing)* That's your problem. *(Pause)* The thought keeps coming back to me, Ed, that there is something particular about this woman. You seem to be protecting her.

Edmund: I think it relates to my experience with Jane (his recently hospitalized daughter). I felt there that I wanted to keep her from hurting. The first impulse, why can't this happen to me rather than to her. *(He relates this to his written evaluation in which he speaks of his growing awareness of the necessity of being with people in pain rather than trying to take the pain away from them and then goes on with the verbatim.)* Part of this is related to my therapy. I had a mother who walked me to school until I was in the third grade. I can remember sitting there in class before the teacher came in. All of the other kids were running around and making noise and my mother was sitting here. In her own way she wanted to be a mother but she was translating mothering into protecting—keeping me from being hurt. And I think that for me, the ministry has been an expression of the same kind of mother. It's been the healing of the hurt and in some ways the cessation of the pain. It's been a struggle to see salvation in terms of process instead of instant change.

Edmund goes on to speak of the contrast in this relationship to a young seminarian counselee and to his forty-four-year-old female counselee. With the male he is more aggressive; with the female he remains hesitant.

Supervisor: I guess I'm wondering what makes you much more hesitant with Ellen.

Edmund: I keep wondering if there is something that's going to happen that I can't control. The conscious answer that comes back to that is, "Probably." The other part is maybe there is no way to avoid that ultimately. If I'm really going to attempt a relationship . . . I find myself saying. If I say that, then this person will say, you're not a good counselor. You're not a good minister. Somehow they would expose the kind of questioning that is still a part of me. It seems like I don't have anything nailed down yet professionally, I feel vulnerable. . . . I've been over at the counseling center about two years, and I still feel like I have a long way to go. It's that kind of personal inadequacy that hurts.

Supervisor: And causes you to protect your counselee. *(Edmund then shares some of his feelings of being higher in the ecclesiastical ladder than some of his collegues in the counseling service, but in terms of confidence being lower than they.)*

Edmund: You know I don't think I expected much to happen with Ellen like I have with my other counselees. I felt like, if it's going to happen, it's going to happen. I just let her set her own pace. It's been a long time since I have played a tape of her for you.

Supervisor: "If mother changes, I won't be the one to do it." It sure makes me want to see how you deal with her when she does come back.

The supervision of Edmund's counseling, like the supervision of traditional clinical pastoral education, involves a focus on the dialogue between his action as a counselor and the being whom he brings into the relationship. A concern with the counselee alone would limit the possibility of Edmund's growth toward a more adequate ministry. His therapy will help, but supervision is in a position to bring professional and personal concerns together. The supervisor puts Edmund in touch with his fear of aggression in his counseling and in his own life. He is protecting his counselee even as he was protected by his mother and in turn protected her by being a good boy, a minister, and even a counselor to middle-aged women. The challenge and support of the supervisor may make it possible for Edmund to "tread loudly" rather than softly and begin to feel his aliveness rather than his carefulness.

Pastoral Consultation

In pastoral consultation, the focus of concern is similar—the minister's quest for unity—the degree of responsibility for the "case," however, is different. The person requesting consultation remains "in charge of the case." The consultant's recommendations may be accepted and acted on or ignored, but final responsibility remains where it was before the consultation. There are many types of consultation.[5] The pastoral consultation I am discussing here is both the type with which I am most familiar and that which I believe is most needed by pastors today.

A consultation group of peers in ministry can be a non-parochial community of faith to which a minister can be accountable, not for the conduct of a particular example of ministry, but for the competency of one's ministry as a whole. Meeting away from their places of ministry with a consultant skilled in dealing with clinical matters of theology and pastoral care, such a group fulfills the need for accountability with respect to matters both personal and confidential, which cannot be dealt with by an official church group. The official group to which a minister is accountable should encourage, if not require, participation in an appropriate consultation group.

The type of consultation I describe here differs from consultation in which a consultant is "brought in" because the consultation in a neutral place tends to focus more on the person asking for help rather than the situation in which help is needed. To be sure, an "on site" consultant can often be used quite effectively. The location, however, significantly changes the nature of the consultation, focusing it more on organizational structure. On-site consultation is generally so close to the job that there is difficulty bringing the more personal issues of faith into dialogue with job function. The best pastoral consultation, as I understand it, occurs when a group of peers who are also in ministry in a place separated from the ministry situation of any of the group members meet with a consultant who understands his or her work as Christian ministry.

The consultation group is a retreat for those for whom the church, or other place of ministry, is as much a place of vulnerability as sanctuary. It is a place where approval may be found, but not a place where the minister has to seek approval. He or she can acknowledge inadequacy and failure without fear of endangering the effectiveness of ministry in that particular place. Such a group is, to use the title of one of Robert Penn Warren's novels, "a place to come to." It is a place to look at one's life, including one's history, in dialogue with the task of ministry.

Pastoral consultation is a means of continuing that life-long quest for putting things together as person and minister. It focuses like pastoral supervision on a person's attempt to bring what he is and what he does together in a meaningful way, but the key issue in pastoral consultation is learning how to ask for and receive help without giving up responsibility for one's life and work.

A skilled pastoral consultant in our pastoral counseling and training center has often said, "What we teach folks is that they are hungry and that they'll be hungry for the rest of their lives." Learning to give and receive pastoral consultation is to be responsive to that basic human hunger: needing other persons and being needed by them.

> The only thing about pastors that may be different from others is that they are often more secret about their emotional dependency, figuring somehow that acknowledging their human condition might reveal a lack of faith. It does, but that's another part of the human condition which we all experience, and acknowledgment seems to help us live with it.[6]

Learning to ask for help is a key element in the process of discovering myself, in staying in touch with the being which I attempt to bring into dialogue with my action. We, at our training center, believe that this is one of the learnings that can be taken from a clinical training process and be capitalized on even when a highly skilled consultant is not available. The consultation seminar, which is a regular part of our training program, therefore is specifically designed to help students learn to ask for what they believe they need.

Part of what it means to be human, we believe, is to learn to get personal help from another human being, not necessarily to act on the counsel given but to experience the availability of help and to use it when appropriate. This understanding of consultation is close in meaning to Tillich's view of ministry and necessarily involves mutuality.[7] One cannot give, he says, unless one is free to receive. Insistence on giving apart from receiving eventually turns the other person into an object and destroys him or her as a person. It also seems close in meaning to Barth's view of essential humanity in which one renders assistance to another in the light of one's own awareness of need.[8]

Pastoral consultation must be distinguished from accumulating information about oneself or suggestions about what one should do in a particular situation. We discourage members of the consultation groups from acting immediately on the consultative responses given them by group members. My colleague and leader of the seminar on consultation, O. L. Delozier, has commented that fresh consultation is like fresh manure. It just smells and doesn't do anyone much good until it ages. This is an earthy way of saying what Kierkegaard put quite differently:

> What good would it do me if truth stood before me, cold and naked, not caring whether I recognized her or not, . . . I certainly do not deny that I still recognize an *imperative of understanding* and that through it one can work upon men, but *it must be taken upon into my life,* and *that is* what I now recognize as the most important thing.[9]

In pastoral consultation one learns that the process of opening up through asking is usually more important than the specific consultative messages received. If I am to learn the truth in a message for me, I will also have to learn not to give an evaluative response to everything that is said to me. The task of the receiver of consultation is to listen carefully, be sure that the message is understood, and then wait for the message to "age"—to see whether it can become a part of the "truth" for him or her.

Another dimension of learning to use consultation is discovering that one can inhibit the immediate impulse to evaluate and classify what has been offered as consultation by another person. Only if this is done can persons risk giving their true perceptions of things. In our training seminar, the person who has asked for help is reminded by the leader simply to listen rather than to offer approval or disapproval to the giver of the consultation. Persons who can begin to do this have learned something of the importance of participating in a community—of acknowledging their dependency on others without immediately experiencing shame because of some apparent inadequacy. They have discovered the value of "a place to come to" where interrelatedness is presupposed and the successes and failures of ministry and life can be discussed with minimum fear of judgment and maximum hope for breaking through personal isolation.

One of the real values of our pastoral care and counseling center is the difficulty that students in the CPE placements have in healing anyone. In the large city hospital where the majority of our students are assigned the volume of human need is so great that students seldom have time to reflect on how they have helped someone before another pressing call is received. In our other placement, a geriatric center with several levels of care, students, rather than struggling with the fact that so much happens that they can't keep up with it, face a situation in which "nothing happens." Older people have an effective way of not "getting better" in spite of one's efforts.

Recently, a student in the latter placement brought some of her discouragement to the consultation seminar. She presented a case in which she had expended a great deal of effort, making effective use of her sensitivity and intelligence, but the woman with whom she had spent so much time refused to get better. All that she had learned about working with people was ineffective. The feeling came through clearly that if she couldn't help "there must be something wrong with her." Her need for some kind of personal reassurance was evident.

A pastoral supervisor might make a variety of responses to this kind of presentation. Perhaps most commonly, he or she would help the student look away from her despair to the case itself and assist her to see both the positive and negative factors in the ministry presented. The supervisor might attempt to relate the ministerial action revealed in the presentation to the student's own personal style, focusing on her implicit quest for unity between the two. In contrast, in the consultation group where she presented this situation, neither the leader, who had over twenty years' experience in pastoral supervision, nor members of the group tried to supervise her.

No one present other than the student herself had any responsibility for her ministry. There was no concerted effort to help her "do it any better." The students who did make such an effort were reminded that the structure of the seminar was to offer whatever they felt personally, not to "help" or to say how they would do it. When they 'id offer their response, the presenter was not allowed to say immediately how she felt about it. That would come later, in the next consultation seminar, after "the manure aged." She was encouraged simply to receive what was offered.

An example of one of the things "received" was a comment by another student who told her, "I don't know how to solve your problem, but what I keep seeing is how you play yourself down—except for your hands. Even when your words talk about how that old lady's dying has defeated you, your hands celebrate life. I'm going to watch your hands."

This incident and one student's remark cannot fully reveal the nature of pastoral consultation. It does, however, illustrate how we attempt to assist pastors in asking for and giving something personal in respose to some of the loneliness of ministry. Certainly, sometimes in consultation what is needed most is a new perspective on "the problem" and how one relates to it. Here consultation is like supervision but without the consultant's responsibility for the ministry performed. In what has been illustrated here, however, consultation is the giving and receiving of a personal response to a colleague's emptiness in offering ministry. "I can't help you with your problem, but I see life in you which perhaps you don't see. In seeing that, I may be able to give you something that direct words of assurance can seldom offer."

Consultation groups can be therapeutic, but may easily be distinguished from psychotherapy. The principle of organization for the group is participation in the work of Christian ministry, not personal problems or desire for character change. Members of the group may bring in personal problems, because in the quest for unity between action and being their person and work are so closely related. Although consultation and supervision have the same focus, in one sense, at least, what is discovered in the consultative process seems prior to what is learned in supervision. Consultation, understood theologically, may be seen as helping persons recover a basic, human capacity which is lost in our estrangement from one another. In learning to give and receive consultation, we relearn our relatedness and partially overcome the shame associated with never having escaped our dependency.

In another sense, consultation comes after supervision. When we have learned through sharing our ministry responsibilities with another more-experienced minister, we graduate to asking for help only when we want it and using only what seems appropriate. There is both an appropriate maturity and an arrogance in this view of consultation. It is good news that I can achieve a professional and personal maturity that makes supervision of my ministry less necessary than it once was. The bad news is that this may suggest to me that there is a private practice of ministry. The nature of humankind and of ministry itself is that any kind of personal ministry apart from involvement in and accountability to community is impossible.

Summary

I have discussed the pastoral counselor's accountability to the communities which confirm and correct his or her ministry both in relation to the Christian communion that ordains him or her and to the communion of professional peers involved in a similar type of ministry. In discussing the former, I have included the pastoral counselor's relationship to the worshiping Christian community which meets to remember and celebrate the Good News of Jesus Christ. In order to be a pastoral counselor, whether in a parish or pastoral counseling center, the minister must be an active participant in such a community.

In addition to participation, however, I have suggested that the pastoral counselor's relationship to the community of faith also involves interpretation and confirmation. His or her interpretation that what is being done in the pastoral counseling ministry is indeed ministry as examined in relation to the ministry of Christ. This is the question for all ministry, not just pastoral counseling. In addition to interpretation by the minister, there must be some confirmation by those in the setting where pastoral counseling is taking place that this work is in at least some way understood and perceived as ministry. The minister's own interpretation of this is not enough. There should be some public confirmation. Pastoral counseling is not a private practice of anything, but is visible and public.

But since much of what is done in pastoral counseling is confidential and cannot be made public, the minister needs relationship to another community, a clinical group of peers in ministry, where confidential matters can be appropriately shared. The visible or sociological church is not structured to do this and needs this additional extra-ecclesial community to facilitate its ministry. I have discussed consultation and supervision at some length, particularly the former, and have attempted to argue that in this clinical community adjunct, but outside the church, something important about Christian community can be discovered and acknowledged—our human hunger and interrelatedness. This can be dealt with ritualistically and symbolically in the visible community, but its personal dimensions are generally denied there and must be expressed elsewhere.

I have noted from the beginning of the chapter that pastoral counseling is not usually a ministry which takes place within the community of faith, but one which, for good reason, takes place outside, though it is significantly related to it. There is a constant danger, therefore, for both the parish minister and the specialist in pastoral counseling that this particular ministry will become a private practice in which he or she is really accountable to no one. For pastoral counseling to continue to be a ministry of the church it must be a not-so-private practice which is continuous with the ministry of Christ.

This completes the major discussion of what pastoral counseling is—an offering of relational humanness sustained by ongoing dialogues with the Christian story, with the identity and role of the minister, and with the community to which the minister is accountable. I turn now to a consideration of some of the significant issues in which pastoral counseling is done, a process which, I believe, throws additional light on what pastoral counseling is. Throughout the discussion, the contributions of clinical material, the dialogue between theology and psychology, and the question of what ministry is will be evident. The first issue is the way one develops a workable structure for pastoral counseling.

Chapter Four

"Magic Questions"—A Working Structure for Pastoral Counseling

Pastoral
Counselor: Hello. This is John Patton.

Caller: I'm Don Smith.* Our pastor, Dr. Ellison, called you and told you about our son needing help.

P.C.: Yes. I remember. I told him that I would be glad to see you if we could find a mutually convenient time, and I also gave him the name of several psychiatrists in case you felt more comfortable with a medically trained psychotherapist.

Caller: My wife and I decided that it would be good for George to see a minister, and Dr. Ellison felt that since the family was so active in the church that it would be better to see someone outside.

P.C: When do you think the family might be able to come in? I have a time available at four next Tuesday. Do you have younger children whom you could bring from school to my office by that time?

C.: Yes. We have three younger children. Two in high school and an eleven-year-old, but we didn't want to involve them in this. What happened—I don't know if Dr. Ellison told you—is that we had to bring George home from military college last week because he was caught smoking pot. I don't think we want the girls and my younger son to know about that.

P.C.: I sure can understand your feeling, but I think it's important that the whole family be involved. If your son's been away from home since fall and suddenly is home again, your whole family has been changed. The

83

*Fictitious name.

> others are affected by his coming home again. I think it's important to acknowledge the change openly.
>
> **C.:** Well, I'm not sure. My wife told me she did not want the younger children to find out why George is home. They have to hear so much about drugs at school. We don't want them to have the same thing at home.
>
> **P.C.:** That makes sense to me. The problem is that I work most effectively when everyone is involved and as much as possible can be talked about openly. Why don't you and your wife talk about what I've said, consider the other therapists you might see, and let me know. I will be glad to see you, but it's important to me to see the whole family at least in the first interview.
>
> **C.:** Well, we'll talk about it and let you know.
>
> **P.C.** Good.
>
> **C.:** Good-bye.
>
> **P.C.:** Good-bye.

Although the names and circumstances have been changed somewhat, most of the issues that are evident in this phone conversation are those with which both the specialist in pastoral counseling and the parish minister must deal at the beginning of counseling. In fact, it begins before the beginning. Pastoral counseling begins with the first contact, with the negotiations about the structure of the relationship. Not enough verbatims have been written about telephone calls inquiring about counseling.

My purpose here is to discuss some of those things that occur at the beginning, or in a sense before the beginning of pastoral counseling. In some way the issues do not fit together logically in terms of their content. They are discussed together here because they occur together in the initial contact or contacts with persons seeking help. The questions are: (1) What is the beginning point in pastoral counseling, and what are the important negotiations associated with the beginning? (2) With whom does one start, or what is the unit of care in pastoral counseling—the individual, the couple, the family?

(3) What kind of initial structuring is done in beginning work with a couple or family? (Dimensions of the latter two questions are examined in both this chapter and the following one.)

Again, the logic of dealing with these questions together is not based as much on their similar content as on the fact that they occur together at the beginning of pastoral counseling. The pastor has to decide how to begin, with whom, and what he or she is about in working with the particular unit of care which has been chosen. Moreover, choosing to do couples or family work does not change pastoral counseling to marriage counseling or family therapy, so that the pastor shifts methodology and theory, or even changes identity. An adequate, not necessarily an exhaustive, pastoral counseling theory is inclusive of whatever unit of care is chosen as appropriate to the situation. Knowing how to begin pastoral counseling includes knowing at least something of how to begin with an individual, couple, or family so that the appropriate unit of care can be dealt with. If, because of lack of time or training, it is then necessary to refer, a better referral can be made and appropriate care can be offered to the whole system needing it, not just to one individual.

Pastoral counseling, for both generalist and specialist, begins with the *asking,* or more accurately, with the dialogue about the asking. In the previous chapter I discussed the importance of learning to ask for help as it applied to the minister's use of consultation. My intention there, as it is here, was to place that process of asking in a positive context, as a dimension of humanness and mutual dependency. It is the same simple and direct expression of human need that we find in the Lord's Prayer where we ask for daily bread, express our anxiety about the temptations of life, and covenant with God to accept the human brokenness of others as he accepts ours.

Initial Structuring Concerns

The first task of the minister in pastoral counseling is to assist persons in recognizing their need for help and affirming their humanness in asking for it. In the telephone conversation with Don Smith the pastoral counselor attempted to do this by hearing a request for help from Don himself as well as for his son. To be sure this way of hearing grew out of the pastor's presupposition about the interrelatedness of family members, but it also was a way of saying to Don, implicitly, "It is quite appropriate and human for you to be asking for help yourself. I hope that you can become comfortable enough with the idea to be more open about it." What the pastor is trying to do, among other things, is to make it possible for Don to choose to be a patient[1] himself rather than just having this arranged for him by his pastor and the pastoral counselor. Whether he is a specialist or generalist in pastoral counseling, some of the pastor's greatest skill is expressed in the process of helping persons acknowledge their need and ask for help to meet it.

For pastors who are intuitively sensitive to other persons' needs or who have, through appropriate training, developed that capacity, there is usually an ongoing battle between sensitivity and seductivity. Although there may be sexual elements in all seductivity, the kind of seductiveness of which I am speaking is usually one that grows out of our need to be needed by others and to be important to them. For the pastoral counselor who is to some degree dependent on fee income for his or her livelihood, the seductivity also has a financial element. Sheldon Kopp, a psychotherapist whose writings have been influential for many of us tells this story:

> When I first began my own private practice I asked a training analyst with whom I was in supervision what my criteria should be for selecting patients. His answer was: "Time enough when you are earning a living and have many to choose from. For now if a gorilla walks into the office with a ten dollar bill clutched in his fist, tell him to lie down on the couch."[2]

Although it is true that the one necessary and sufficient condition for psychotherapy, pastoral or otherwise, is a client, there is an important ethical issue here both for the pastor who is compensated for his or her counseling by fee income and the one who offers counseling on salaried time. This may or may not be the best time for a particular person, couple, or family to get help, and I may or may not be the person who can most effectively offer that help. Although for reasons of personal gratification (needing to be needed—or finance (producing additional income), I may want this person for a counselee, I have an ethical responsibility not to seduce him or her into counseling in order to satisfy my own needs. I have talked to few pastors who have not at one time or another been ethically irresponsible on this issue. When offered before its time, counseling, like wine, is seldom worth what is paid for it, whether the fee is money, time, or special attention.

In the Don Smith telephone call, the pastoral counselor attempted to get at the issue of choice by reminding the caller that he has given Don's pastor the names of several other therapists and that the choice was still open. He encouraged him to talk it over with his wife and, in effect, to take responsibility for his choice. If Don, then, accepts the appointment with the pastoral counselor, he will more clearly have chosen this for himself and his family rather than just following the recommendation of his pastor. That choice will be something that the counselor can build on as he attempts to get Don in touch with his responsibility for his life.

There is an interesting dialectic here, one that is often experienced as a conflict. On one hand the pastor, specialist or generalist, is expected to be sensitive and available, reaching out to persons in need. On the other hand, if an essential part of the counseling process is the way it begins, with the person needing help reaching out and asking for it, then for the pastor to reach out too far is to undercut the counselee's initiative and undermine the counseling process. Counselors need to assert their availability and then wait for a choice to be made by the person seeking help.

There are many people whom I have learned from a

colleague to think of as "sneaky feeders," those who manage to get something from just being around. They are not unlike the woman who touched the hem of Jesus' garment, preferring not to acknowledge her need for pastoral care or other specific dimensions of the church's ministry. They get something of what they need without having to acknowledge who they are or what they need. More is possible with choice and acknowledgement, and the pastor or caring layperson may help persons move in that direction by not attempting to sell the wine before its time and appreciating the value to some of just sniffing the aroma.

The second task for the beginning of pastoral counseling is that of conducting the interview under the best possible circumstances. Pastoral counseling can be conducted in the back seat of a convertible, but it is not likely to be the best counseling that the pastor is capable of doing in a more appropriate setting. Certainly, one of the strengths of pastors' role, in contrast to that of other helping persons, is that they can offer care without high overhead expenses. This tradition of flexibility, however, may often be responsible for the pastor's offering less than professional care. Whether the prospective counselee seeks help from a parish minister or a pastoral counseling specialist, he or she has the right to expect to come to a comfortable place, which offers freedom from interruption and in some way demonstrates the confidentiality of the counseling process. Pastors who cannot offer this should not engage in much counseling.

Likewise, pastors themselves need to work in comfortable and familiar circumstances which are relatively free from distracting noises and reminders of other responsibilities. Those who engage in pastoral counseling in the parish and in pastoral counseling centers need to work with the appropriate committees and boards in order to secure such favorable working conditions. Although it is important to affirm the pastor's historic initiative in reaching out to persons rather than waiting for them to come to the church or agency, it is equally important to recognize the value of a person going somewhere to get help. Persons who modify their routine to schedule appointments in a place away from work or home are much more likely to secure help than those who take less initiative and find a way to get the counselor to come to them. The anxiety raised in that process of going somewhere for counseling will make persons more able to use the counseling process.

The third task for the beginning of pastoral counseling is dealing sensitively with the anxiety that has been raised by the person who comes for counseling. I have found no better practical guide for this than in the clinical work of Harry Stack Sullivan and in his understanding of what constituted an "expert in interpersonal relations."[3] Sullivan described such persons as sensitive, able to offer security in relationships, and straightforward, concrete, and simple in their communication. One example of this type of approach can be seen in Sullivan's description of his initial encounter with the patient. He began by telling what he knew thus far about why the person had come. If the patient had phoned to make the appointment, Sullivan gave a brief summary of that conversation in a simple, matter-of-fact way in order to let the person know what he knew and didn't know. He found, and this has been confirmed in my own experience, that such a procedure lets the person know where the counselor is with him or her and that the process of the interview is going to be similarly simple and direct. The intent in this initial interaction as well as with much of the subsequent interview is to recognize the anxiety of the person seeking help and to deal with it by letting the counselee know as soon as possible how the counselor will be functioning. This tends to relieve some of the anxiety by suggesting that the counselor knows what he or she is doing and also encourages the counselee to follow a similar direct, straightforward procedure insofar as he or she is able to do. With couples and families, this is particularly helpful, because it conveys the feeling that the counselor has not made a secret pact with anyone and that he or she intends to let all of them in on what is going on.

The "Magic Questions"

After making an attempt to recognize and, in some way, deal with the initial anxiety of the person or persons coming for counseling, the pastoral counselor can move directly into the task of structuring some of the early contents of the counseling interview. In my experience this is most effective when one makes use of what have sometimes been called "the magic questions." Raising these questions and beginning to deal with them is the fourth task in the beginning of pastoral counseling. Virtually every staff conference I have ever attended, whether in a psychiatric, psychological, or pastoral counseling setting, made use of these questions in discussing cases. What is "magic" about them is that they provide focus and perspective on almost any situation, enabling one to know at least something about how to deal with it. Curiously, like magic powers that are sometimes part of familiar fairy tales, they are often forgotten. The function of a consultation group or a supervisor is to remind pastoral counselors that they can use the questions to achieve clarity and direction.

I recall an incident when our psychiatric consultant first began to see a few patients at the pastoral counseling center as well as in his private office. He decided that it was appropriate for him to present some of his cases for consultation just as the pastoral counselors did. His first case was presented with a multitude of facts, including some interesting religious features. The psychiatrist confessed that in spite of all this information, he was having difficulty deciding what to do with the patient. Then one of the pastoral counselors asked, "What is *she* looking for?" Our consultant gave an embarrassed smile and said, "I forgot to ask."

He forgot to ask the magic questions: What is the counselee looking for? Why did this person pick this particular time to ask for help? Why did he or she come here or come to me? In the midst of all the detailed misery that people share with us, I am almost embarrassed to bring up questions as simple as these. Perhaps that is why I too forget them. It seems like a "wise professional person" such as myself should be able to figure out what is needed, but it is just that expectation of myself that gets in the way of my hearing or asking what a person wants. My need to help may get in the way of the counselee's intentionality, his own way for formulating what seems possible in this impossible situation. My own perceptiveness in seeing all the things that were wrong may get in the way of my identifying the few things that we may be able to do something about. The first magic question is most important because it puts responsibility for the counseling process in the right place—with the counselees—and frees me to help them carry out their responsibility for what they believe can be changed. (How this question is used in the diagnostic process is discussed in chaper 6.)

The second question, Why now? helps mobilize the urgency and the sense of possibility that the counselee bring. Whatever the problem is, in all likelihood, it started long ago. Counselees come in now because they have perceived a change—in the situation, in the possibility of getting help, or in some other way. If something has changed, it can change again, and therein lies the possibility of the counselees getting help. They were able to see something they had not seen before. If they can see that, they can see other things which may produce some different types of changes. It was not explicitly stated in the phone conversation, but if Don Smith's son George got caught smoking pot at college, in all probability he had been smoking at home as well. The previous circumstances were not uncomfortable enough to bring George's relationship to the family into question. The present situation gives an opportunity to do that. The family wants to change something that probably needed changing before now, but had not found the right time yet. The second magic question gets at both the fact of change and the possibility of another change.

The third question, Why me or why this place? begins the process of talking openly about relationship. It is intended to facilitate the formation of what a number of writers about psychotherapy have called, "forming the therapeutic alliance." It places emphasis on the healing factor in the pastoral counseling process—however long that process may be—the relationship. Beginning pastoral counselors, and other types of therapists as well, usually are more embarrassed about asking this question than they are asking the other two. It seems to set up a situation in which the counselee will compliment the pastor, and it is not good manners we have learned, to ask for compliments. Pastoral counseling is not a situation, however, in which the usual social conventions apply. However inadequate we as counselors may actually be, to the person who has come for help, we are very important. Part of the task in learning pastoral counseling, in fact, one of the most important parts, is learning to talk relatively comfortably about the counseling relationship and the counselor's importance to the counselee. This issue is discussed at length in chapter 7. My concern here is to affirm that the importance of the pastoral relationship begins at the beginning, and sometimes, for the parish minister, it begins before the counseling. It is here that pastors first make use of the fact that, before the first word is said, they are more important to the counselee than simple observation can explain.

Each of the magic questions reaches deeply into the meaning of the counseling process. The counselee's responsibility for asking for what he or she needs, the implicit hope for change present in the perception that things are different now, and the affirmation of belief that some kind of healing is possible, all have meanings which, from the perspective of faith, are theological. My concern, however, is not to explore these meanings now, but to continue the practical discussion of the beginning of pastoral counseling by describing other important ways of structuring the counseling situation. Other elements of the structuring process are discussed later in this chapter and in the two subsequent chapters. My concern here is to explore the pastor's responsibility for determining how the interview will be conducted. I do this in terms of two concepts: limiting and listening. The exact relationship between the two concepts is still not clear to me, but I am convinced that within the counseling process each is facilitated by the other.

Limiting and Listening

The setting up of the pastoral counseling interview is itself a limiting feature of structure. The relationship is in some way limited to that particular period of time. Because of that limit, some things are possible which are not possible in ordinary social relationships. Because the pastoral counseling is relating to a certain person primarily during a particular period of time, an intensiveness is possible which would not be if the relationship went on indefinitely. The pastoral counselor is not responsible for the counselee's whole life, only for an hour or so on a periodic basis, but in that limited time, the counselor's resonsibility is to help the counselee see what is real and important and make some judgments about it.

A significant problem for both generalists and specialists in pastoral counseling is learning to set limits in their relationship to counselees. Anyone who has supervised beginning pastoral counseling students has heard, "The best part is not on the tape. It was when we went overtime and the tape had run out." The inexperienced pastoral counselor, whatever setting he or she works, has difficulty accepting and imposing limits. If she just allowed a little more time something important would happen. Or the counselee who says, "I just don't think I can get started in an hour. Could I have double sessions?" This all seems quite reasonable, except for the fact that life itself is limited, and part of learning to live involves discovering and accepting the limits in a particular situation. The ability of the pastoral counselor to set and use limits is an important element in his or her ability to be useful to people.

When clear limits of time are effectively adhered to, the pastoral counselor is free to listen fully within the limited time available. Virtually all the psychotherapies are predicated on the ability of the counselor to listen actively to what is being said by the counselee. The major influences on modern pastoral counseling, Hiltner's educative method[4] and Rogers' client-centered counseling[5] have helped us develop ways of doing this. Truax and Carkhuff's skill training have furthered this development[6] as has Gendlin's experiential focusing.[7] Perhaps most important in all the recent work on listening is the reminder that listening is an active process.[8] One cannot simply sit silently and passively and be able to stay awake, much less understand what is being said. The pastoral counselor must find some balance between hearing a person's story in his or her own words and structuring the story so that it connects with the counselor's own and, thus, be remembered and understood. It is important, as Rogers emphasized, that we attempt to understand the internal framework of the client, but we do this best, as he later emphasized,[9] when we know and use our own to resonate with that of the client.

This is where listening and limiting move into some dialectical relationship. It is important to listen, but not to more material than can be reasonably understood. Faking it is counterproductive, because it gradually destroys an honest relationship. The pastoral counselor, therefore, will openly acknowledge his or her limits in understanding and reveal these limits as a way of facilitating dialogue rather than restricting it.

In addition to the fact that listening should be limited in order to make the counseling process easier for the counselor, listening should also be limited to make things easier for the counselee. Because most pastors have learned to minister to persons in the crisis of death and illness before they learn pastoral counseling, it is often difficult for them to accept the fact that they can listen to too much. The opportunity for catharsis is essential in crisis ministry. Telling too much of the story in the first interview may actually delay the process of the whole story being told. The anxiety that acts as a dynamic for the counseling process may be too dissipated for the counseling to proceed, or the counselee may tell too much before the relationship is perceived as trustworthy enough to contain what has been told.

The pastoral counselor must learn to use his or her sensitivity to the relationship between content being told and degree of relationship formed to limit or encourage the counselee in telling what needs to be told. Being out of touch with this delicate balance can lead to the embarrassment of the counselee and the premature termination of the relationship. More of this is discussed later when we consider the diagnostic process as another means of structuring.

We have now considered some of the important issues involved in the beginning of the counseling process whether it is with an individual, couple, or family. They are some of the issues that must be dealt with by the beginning pastoral counselor in whatever setting he or she may work. My concern now is to move to the important question of structuring pastoral counseling through determining the unit of the care—the number of persons to be seen at the beginning and later in the counseling process.

The Unit of Care

When does the minister decide to work with a couple rather than an individual, and is it the minister who decides this? Because the minister is responsible for setting the structure of the interview or interviews, he or she is the one to decide this as a part of the general problem of establishing the optimum conditions for the counseling. Both the parish minister and the pastoral counseling specialist are tempted to handle this matter otherwise, simply to give in to what the counselee wants. What the counselee usually wants is to be seen alone at first, and that means, very humanly, "I want you to help my marriage, but I want you to see it from my point of view."[10] And the counselee intuitively knows that if he is seen alone, the pastor will do just that—in spite of all his or her protestations to the contrary.

If, as is usually the case, the counselee is from outside the membership of the parish and if he or she is married the pastor as well as the pastoral counseling specialist can proceed by insisting that both husband and wife come in for the first interview. If the person is a parishioner, the minister can suggest that both members of the couple come in, but because the parishioner has some right to the pastor's time as an individual, the parishioner can influence the structure of the initial interview. After that, however, even with a parishioner, if the marriage has been discussed in any way (and in virtually every case it has been) the spouse should be included. If not, the minister may have unknowingly begun an emotional affair with the counselee that may be ultimately destructive to the marriage relationship.

I am aware that this is a strong, perhaps dogmatic, statement. If it is true, however, as I believe it is, that pastoral counseling, which goes beyond the initial evaluation of the situation, is appropriately an intimate emotional experience, then, unless it takes place with the participation of the spouse, it is usually competitive with the marriage. In order to avoid this and, more positively, to allow the person's pain to be dealt with within the context of the marriage relationship, a conversation like the following is appropriate:

Caller: Rev. Patton, this is Joyce Osment (fictitious name). I would like to come in and talk to you.

Pastoral Counselor: Are you free to tell me a little of what it's about over the phone?

Caller: I'd rather not. I'm at the office, and this is not a good place to talk. Do you have any time this week?

P.C.: My usual practice is to see married persons together with their spouse. Are you married?

C.: Yes, I am, but this doesn't really concern my husband—at least not directly.

P.C.: I see. My experience has been that both members of a marriage should be present the first time I see a married person. It helps me to understand the situation better and enables the less-involved person to know who I am.

C.: I would like that, but there are some things that it would be easier for me to talk about without my husband there, and it would also be hard for him to get off from work.

P.C.: I've discovered that, for me at least, it's more important to see something of the relationship the first time I meet with someone than it is to hear their personal secrets. That can come later if you feel like I'm the kind of person you would want to tell them to. Let me ask you to do this. Talk with your husband. Tell him to come in the first time, at least, and see what he says. Call me back tomorrow or the next day and let me know.

C.: *(Apparently somewhat irritated)* I already know what he'll say. He won't come.

P.C.: I know that you probably do know what he'll say, but try it anyway. Tell him that it's just my way of doing things, and maybe he will understand. Call me back tomorrow and tell me what he said.

C.: Well, all right, but I already know what will happen.

P.C.: I'll look forward to hearing about it tomorrow.

I have participated in some version of this dialogue literally hundreds of time, and I am convinced that it is as important as most of the counseling I have done. A number of issues come out rather clearly in such a conversation. The pastor would like to hear "a little" of what Ms. Osment is concerned about. If she acknowledges at the outset that the problem relates to her marriage, the pastor is in a better position to get her to acknowledge that her husband should come in. She avoids this, so he moves to his central argument based on what his usual practice is. It is obviously to the counselee's advantage for him to follow his usual practice. He has more experience in working that way and that should help him to be more effective. The pastor indicates early in the call that he wants Ms. Osment's spouse to know who he is and how he works. If she does decide to come in, their relationship is not going to be secretive. In fact, he attempts to make it clear that, in the kind of counseling he does, relationships are more important than secrets anyway. Thus the pastor has shared one of his central beliefs even before he meets the counselee, that knowing persons seldom comes from knowing things about them.

The pastor takes a strong stand in structuring the first interview. He literally tells the prospective counselee what to do—talk to her husband. In doing so, he is attempting to teach one of the major goals of pastoral counseling, namely, that the counselee should learn to talk more effectively with his or her significant other. Interestingly, she says that she doesn't really need to do this because she already knows what he will say—probably not only about this matter but about everything. The pastor does not argue, but restates his request as if he assumes that the husband can speak for himself and indicates when he expects her to call back.

This kind of firm structuring is important in setting up the best conditions under which a pastoral counseling interview can take place. If these conditions are clear and firm, then the counselees are more likely to feel that the pastoral counselor knows what he/she is doing, even though they may not like all of it. A pastoral counselor who is this directive in setting conditions for the interview may have to find ways later on to interpret to counselees that he/she is in charge of the interview, not of their lives. A firm structure for counseling makes it more likely for them to believe this than counseling that begins with an "anything goes" kind of philosophy.

Changing the Structure

When does the pastoral counselor change the structure for counseling and agree to see a married person without the spouse? Probably more often than he or she should. It is simply easier to do what someone wants than to hold one's position on the best way for conducting the interview. Both the parish minister and the pastoral counseling specialist may worry about not being liked or fear rejection by the potential counselee. If fees make up a significant portion of the pastor's income, he or she risks financial loss in holding the line. After working this way for over fifteen years, I am convinced that a good deal more is gained than lost in insisting on seeing both parties.

From what we have heard thus far from Joyce Osment, it would be inappropriate to give into her wishes and modify the structure. She apparently wants counseling apart from her husband, so that she can deal with things that are secret from him or things that she perceives would hurt him. For the pastor to modify the couple's interview structure at the beginning of the counseling would be to become a part of the secrets and, in effect, to encourage an emotional affair with Joyce, whether or not either he or she had any such intent.

The reason for this has little or nothing to do with the intentions of either pastoral counselor or counselee. Pastoral counseling at its best in an intense emotional relationship. It takes place under circumstances that are confidential. It is because of this that it should be entered into with the knowledge and support of both parties in the marriage so that the emotional exchange which takes place in the pastoral counseling can contribute to the strength of the marriage rather than undermine it. By insisting on the couple's structure for counseling, the pastor affirms the importance of the marriage in the midst of Ms. Osment's despair about it. The pastor *acts* as if the marriage were important rather than telling the couple how important it is. This leaves him free to work with the individuation of each member of the couple within the context of the marriage rather than apart from it.

The pastor can appropriately see one member of a marriage, however, when the counselee wants to have the spouse involved, but does not have the negotiating power to accomplish it. If the use of the pastoral counselor's own power fails to accomplish this—as was suggested to Ms. Osment in telling her husband that it was the counselor's idea, not hers, to have the husband come in—it is appropriate to see the individual spouse alone. Even under these circumstances, however, it is important to recognize the seductive power of the counselee's helplessness. When both members of a couple are present the pastoral counselor is free to become involved emotionally with each person's pain and to understand the relationship. When only one is present, counseling is restricted to helping that person deal with his or her own feelings, separating them from the confusion of the marital situation and beginning to identify what can and cannot be changed.

(After a relationship with a couple has been established, working with individuals becomes a different issue related to another part of the counseling process. See chapter 5.)

When seeing a married counselee alone, there are two important structuring actions of the initial counselor. I discuss more of the actual content of the initial interview in the following chapter. My concern here is in the structuring, whatever content is expressed. The first of these actions is the pastoral counselor's insistence that the counselee talk about his or her own feelings, not what the spouse has done. Obviously, it is impossible to separate these completely. The counselee cannot talk about his or her own feelings without also talking about the spouse. The pastor's structuring is an effort to get the emphasis in the most useful place, not to rule out all material about the husband. A clinical example may be useful. It is hypothetical and condensed for emphasis:

P.C.: Tell me about how you happened to come in to see me. What was going on in your life that was painful?

C.: My husband is never at home. He leaves at five o'clock in the morning and rarely comes home until six or seven in the evening. On the weekend he hunts or fishes. I just don't see him anymore.

P.C.: And what are your feelings about this?

  C: I don't feel married. He doesn't seem to care about anything except being with his hunting friends. The little time he is at home he's drinking beer in front of the television.

P.C.: I'm not sure what you are feeling about this. You sound angry.

  C.: I am, but I don't know what to do. Whenever I try to tell him how I feel, he doesn't say anything, but just walks away. He's not doing well in his job.

P.C.: Try to tell me what your feelings are. I hear some of your anger. You sound like you feel powerless or something like that.

  C.: I can't do a thing. Of course I feel powerless. What's wrong with him? That's what I want to know.

P.C.: I thought you were asking what's wrong with you.

  C.: There's nothing wrong with me. Or I don't think so. I'm the one who's interested in sex, not him. He's too tired or he hurt his back. There's always something to keep him away from me.

P.C.: Jim's been successful at staying away from both of us. I don't think even my guesses about him will be very accurate unless I can get to know you better. Try to tell me how what Jim does affects you—what kind of feelings it stirs up in you.

  C.: *(Long pause)* I think I feel ashamed.

The primary concern of the pastor in this interview is in getting at the counselee's pain, her feelings about her life situation. She insistently talks about what is wrong with her husband, Jim. The pastor on the other hand ignores most of this, neither asking questions about it or reflecting on the content of what she says about him. Rather, he insistently comes back to her feelings. In reading the interview, the pastor may appear naïve. Some of the things he asks seem obvious. It seems that he should know how the counselee feels, if he is as sensitive and understanding as he is expected to be. And yet if he knows or assumes he knows, the counselee will never have the opportunity to tell him who she is by saying what she feels. Everything will be a description of the "bad" husband. The pastor and the counselee will shake their heads sadly about how bad the husband is and nothing will be done to change things. The counselee will remain undifferentiated from the husband's problems which, because he is not here, cannot be dealt with directly anyway.

If, however, the counselee can learn to talk about herself, to experience her own feelings, and not attributing everything important she feels to her husband, she may then begin to experience some power and choice about her life. This sounds like a long process, and in many ways it is. On the other hand, in just one or two encounters where her feelings rather than her husband's behavior are emphasized, she may begin to discover that there is more than one way to experience and understand her life. For the pastor this involves a rather aggressive, intervening, sometimes almost combative, approach. The pastor's goal may be to be educative or client-centered, but to get there may seem to involve a fight. My contention is that this can be a very useful, respectful, caring sort of fight.

The second structuring action which the pastor tries to accomplish in meeting alone with a married person is focusing on what the counselee has done about his or her painful life situation. Feelings, awareness and expression of what one feels, lead to some differentiation from the circumstances of life and perhaps to a sense of some power to change them. The counselor focusing on what has been done or what the counselee is planning to do furthers that process and nourishes any sense of freedom and power that may emerge. When the counselee complains about the situation or about the spouse, the pastor responds with interest in her action or intended action. If progress in moving from complaint to feeling has been made during the interview, the pastor can begin to respond in terms of action rather than focusing on feeling. For example:

> C: He was gone all weekend, and he left me a note this morning saying he wouldn't be home tonight.

P.C.: And what have you planned to do about this?

   C: I don't know. I just feel so helpless.

P.C.: I think I understand something of how you feel, but I don't know yet what you are doing about those feelings.

   C: Nothing, I guess. I don't know what to do.

P.C.: Well, you did come here and perhaps you are a bit clearer about how you feel about all this. That's a first step. Does he know that you've come here to get something for yourself?

   C.: I don't know. I think I told him it had to do with the marriage.

P.C.: I really don't know how to be very useful to the marriage without his being here with you, so I've been assuming that what you were about was changing yourself. It's possible that he might be willing to come in to help you with that.

   C.: I'll try and tell him.

P.C.: I feel pretty sure that you can get the message across if you really want to. You've managed to share your hurt and some of your need to change with me. If you can do it here, you can eventually do it at home too.

   C.: How do I do it?

P.C.: I have been able to understand you when you talked about yourself and not him. I suspect that he and I are more alike than you think.

This part of the interview focuses on action, that something is being done and can be done. The counselee is offered support, but without any commiserating about how bad the situation is or any implicit, "You poor thing." The support is in the form of a reminder of what already has been done and the suggestion through implication that she can do what she needs to do. If this message comes only in words of reassurance, it will probably be rejected because it is too far removed from the counselee's way of looking at things. If, on the other hand, it is simply assumed as the way things are, the counselee will have to surrender her passivity and aggressively contradict the counselor's assumption about her competence to do what needs to be done. In either case, she has given up her stance of relating through helplessness and given the counselor new opportunity to focus on her responsibility and ability to choose.

In dealing with a married person without his or her spouse, then, the pastoral counselor needs to make extensive use of structuring. The focus is first on feelings and then action, to the end that the counselee will begin to experience herself as having feelings and the capacity for action which are not determined by the painful life situation. The pastor in this kind of counseling situation acts much like a consultant, reducing his or her involvement with the counselee, and attempts to strengthen the counselee's capacities to deal with the situation outside the counseling hour. This type of counseling will be limited to a very few interviews. Otherwise, it will become more important and emotionally satisfying to the counselee than what happens in the real life situation, more like an emotional affair than a useful consultation.

I have attempted in this chapter to deal with what happens at the beginning of pastoral counseling and, actually, before the beginning. In doing so, I have called attention to the initial structuring of the counseling process, attempting to underscore its importance. Although it has not been sufficiently emphasized, such structuring is not in opposition to what has been presented in the literature of pastoral counseling about caring, attentive listening. It is a way of setting up the conditions under which such listening can be most effective.

The emphasis of the chapter has been on specific elements of the practice of pastoral counseling rather than its theoretical and theological base. Throughout the discussion, however, the pastor's visibility, his or her openness and willingness to be seen as pastor has been evident. The pastor's ability to move with strength is based on a firm pastoral identity and a clear-cut accountability for what he or she is doing. Personal authority is evident in the case material, but also evident is the authority of the pastoral office and accountability to something other than to one's self and one's client.

I have suggested some of the theological assumptions in the so-called "magic questions" of structuring. More of this is developed later in the chapter on diagnosis. The structuring dimensions of determining the unit of care also reveal important assumptions about the human condition. In the case examples given, although the pastor emphasized effectiveness of function rather than his beliefs about human relatedness, implicit theological messages about the importance of commitment and covenant were communicated in the structuring process. More of this is developed in the chapter that follows. Most important, in subsequent chapters as some of the technical procedures of the counseling process are discussed and developed, the attempt is made to show how these can be understood as pastoral procedures, significantly related to the role, identity and accountability of the pastor as well as to the secular counseling theory in which they are sometimes presented.

Chapter Five

System and Person—The Unit of Care in Pastoral Counseling

I attempted in the previous chapter to demonstrate the importance of structuring the counseling situation in order to create the optimum conditions under which to offer relationship. Perhaps the most important element in that structuring is determining and working with the appropriate unit of care. With persons who are living with a marital partner or family, that unit of care is usually the couple or the entire family. The request for help from a person who is living in a family carries with it, at least implicitly, the question, What are the assumptions about marriage and family that influence the way you offer care? Discussions of such presuppositions are not, therefore, out of place in a consideration of the beginning phase of pastoral counseling.

Most of the material in this chapter concerns the theory and method of working with persons in families. It is presented here, however, in the context of addressing further the question, What is the appropriate unit of care for pastoral counseling? One can deal with individuals within families when the reality of the marriage and family have been addressed at the beginning of the process. It is much more difficult to move from what was begun as an individual pastoral counseling relationship to working with the couple and family.

For over ten years I taught pastoral care and counseling in a four-week course for United Methodist pastors who, for one reason or another, were unable to go to seminary. The concerns of these pastors were far more practical than theoretical. They were at work in the field without adequate training, and they knew it. Their questions were simple and direct and often included something like this, "How do I do marriage counseling with a couple like that?" My response to the questions were similarly direct and frequently it was, "Don't worry about being a marriage counselor. Do what you already know something about. Be a pastor—to the couple or to the whole family." My purpose in this chapter is to develop that point of view both theoretically and practically.

Pastoral counseling with couples and families is of a piece with the pastoral counseling of individuals. One does not surrender the pastoral perspective when the unit of care includes more than one person. What the pastor offers is essentially the same whatever the unit of care. It is what we have called relational humanness—a genuinely human presence and the capacity to offer that presence under a variety of circumstances. When a pastor works with a couple or family instead of an individual, it is not necessary to change from one theory and methodology of care to another. Rather, additional theory and methods are added to enrich an already existing understanding of the pastoral relationship. The practical implication of this point of view is to encourage pastors, whatever level of competency in counseling they possess, to build on what they already have, namely, some capacity to offer pastoral care to persons and to offer that in relation to marriage and family systems as well as to individuals.

If the theological norm for pastoral counseling is relational humanness, patterned in some way after the humanness of Christ for us, then the purpose of pastoral counseling with couples or families cannot be to "save" the marriage or to return the family to the condition in which it existed prior to the development of the "problem." The purpose is to offer something new—the kind of relationship that will intervene creatively in the marital or family system so that the persons within it will experience some freedom to change, to consider some new alternatives about their lives. Each individual within the system will experience some needed care and, because of it, will be able to go on about his or her life with less baggage than each had been carrying before.

Covenant and Commitment

Much has been written about family systems, and it is not necessary to repeat that discussion here.[1] The point of view developed in this chapter is that it is possible to take both system and individual seriously in a way comparable to the biblical understanding of the individual in community. "In the covenant with the nation God dignified each member with his personal address, so that each one understood the responsible nature of his relationship to the Divine Person. The Lord of the nation was also the Lord of each of its individuals."[2] "In the Bible," says Walter Brueggemann, " 'person' means to belong with and belong to and belong for. Covenant is thus deeply set against every notion of human autonomy."[3] What I have discussed in chapter 1 as "neighbor-hood," revealed in the New Testament through the work of the Christ, points to both the importance of the individual—the neighbor to be served—and of the family system, which must be understood and dealt with if service is to be relevant and appropriate.

The biblical understanding of humankind argues for a pastoral response to a person to take place within the system of relationships to which they have joined themselves in covenant—to their spouse in the service of marriage and to their children in the vows associated with the sacrament of baptism. These services emphasize the importance of family relationship "in the sight of God" and recognize that both family system and individual are the objects of pastoral concern. The seriousness of family relationships, however, does not mean that they should be idealized or romanticized as some of the literature on premarital counseling, marriage enrichment, and the like seems to do.[4]

There is within scripture a useful corrective to this—a more balanced and realistic view which may be seen in the contrasting emphases of the following texts: "It is not good that the man should be alone" (Gen. 2:18) and "For in the resurrection they neither marry nor are given in marriage" (Matt. 22:30). One suggests the importance of intimate relationship; the other, its temporality.

My argument is not that these two texts "prove" anything, but that they present a dialectic that is representative of biblical thought as a whole. The Bible takes marriage and the family seriously, but not too seriously. The symbol of the resurrection reminds us that God's covenant transcends all human covenants. A Christian view of marriage insists on both the development of individual personhood and the growth that is possible only in an intimate relationship of commitment and continuity.[5]

> In both Old and New Testaments, commitment and continuity of relationship are seen not so much as referent to marriage as to the very nature of God. In spite of human inconsistency and unfaithfulness, God gives himself in a binding, future-oriented involvement with a particular people. The theme of divine promise, of fulfillment and meaning, is a central message of the Bible. Human response involves faith in this promise in spite of massive evidence of meaninglessness and temporality. Human relationships, then, are to be undertaken with a spirit similar to that of God's covenant with persons in Christ. Like that covenant, they involve a commitment to affirm another person in spite of his or her sin, and a willingness to struggle together toward a future that is ultimately in God's hands.
>
> This kind of personal commitment involves a willingness to allow marriage to be viewed not only for what it appears to be, but also as a part of God's larger history with his people. The marriage relationship, defined by the larger context of God's covenant, must be free to grow and develop in new and unexpected ways and to be judged ultimately by God and his loving purposes. Marriage, viewed from this perspective, involves a willingness to celebrate the commitment between a man and a woman as an occasion for living fully under the covenant which God has given.

A development or extension of the meaning of our first text, then, in the light of this understanding of commitment and covenant, would be: "It is good for men and women to be committed to one another in a marriage relationship because in such a relationship they not only relieve their loneliness, but partially exemplify or illustrate God's commitment to persons and their ultimate value." A development of the second text would be, "Although a committed human relationship reveals something of the character of God, no human relationship is permanent. One which becomes an end in itself obscures the freedom and destiny of the person suggested by the symbol of resurrection. Each person is ultimately related through Christ to God alone." Both individual personhood, viewed as having eternal significance in the light of God's covenant, and the importance of committed relationships are at the heart of the biblical message.

My assumptions, then, about marriage and the family, in the light of this understanding of commitment and covenant, are that these institutions are important, but not eternal. Marriage and the family grow out of a very practical human problem, loneliness, and should not be romanticized or elevated in importance. They should, rather, be seen as major opportunities for the development of personhood in the light of God's affirmation of us and our commitment to each other. Such relationships should, therefore, be entered into and exited from "discreetly, advisedly, soberly, and in the fear of God," and, sometimes, with the assistance of a competent pastoral counselor. (From an article in *Openings into Ministry* edited by Ross Snyder)

Seeing the System Firsthand

The view of marriage and the family that I have presented has several implications for pastoral counseling. The first has to do with the specific concern of this chapter, the unit of care to which pastoral counseling is offered. Following the biblical analogy, just as God in covenant is related to the individual in community, so the pastor is called to offer care both to the marital or family system and to the individuals within it. The pastoral counseling of couples and families must respond both to the person who asks for help and to the system of which he or she is a part—even when the person asking for help seems to be leaving out the marital partner or other members of the family. The telephone conversations with Don Smith and Joyce Osment mentioned earlier illustrate this. For one reason or another, the callers are resistive to involving the family or spouse. Sometimes they simply do not know that it is done that way. The image of the confessional with the individual or the psychoanalyst and his patient are still operative in forming people's expectations. The pastor does not disregard this, but attempts to broaden the image of how help may be received.

The reader may wish to refer to the chapter on structuring, particularly to the clinical material dealing with the unit of care. The intent in that chapter was to insist on the importance of the pastor's structuring the counseling process rather than dealing with it more or less passively. The illustrations chosen were those which are most frequent in my experience, when the pastoral counselor must remind the person who calls for help that the best help will come if spouse and/or family are involved. Within the context of a discussion on structuring, the important issue is the pastor's winning the battle of doing counseling under the best possible circumstances. Within the context of a discussion on the pastoral counseling of couples and families, the important issue is the unit of care itself.

The pastor needs to be related directly to the whole system under stress, not just hear about it secondhand. If the whole system is available, it does not mean that the pastor will see everyone together each time. The primary concern is to see that the marital or family system is not subverted and that the pastoral counseling relationship does not become a substitute for it. In such a case, the pastoral counseling will almost surely fail, because the pastor has substituted an unreal situation (the counseling) for a real one and has become part of a person's life in a way that cannot continue.

To put it more pointedly, the pastor who fails to take a marital system seriously enough to make every effort to have both spouses involved in the counseling may naïvely be providing an emotional affair for the spouse who is involved. He or she is contributing to the counselee's disloyalty to the marital system in a way that is ultimately destructive.[6] As I suggested earlier, only under circumstances where the spouse has been consulted and at least involved in the decision about counseling can the pastor work with one member of a couple without competing in some way with the marital system.

The Uniqueness of the Marriage Relationship

Another practical implication of the view of marriage that I have taken has to do with the wisdom of marital choice. Particular marriages are not made in heaven, but the choice of a marriage partner goes far beyond conscious decision. The general understanding of covenant involves active choice and agreement, but it is also based on the fact that God chose us prior to our ability to respond to him. Marital choice is also based on something deeper than conscious decision. John Warkentin, speaking for a group of colleagues who have pioneered in working therapeutically with couples, has said:

> The exquisite accuracy of marital pairing of personality character-istics repeatedly impresses us. However, we are aware that the partners may be less than well-matched in terms of social background, religious affiliation, educational achievement, and even basic intellectual capacity. However, their unconscious styles of life are almost certainly in close agreement, at least as far as we therapists can determine.[7]

One does not have to understand exactly how this unconscious wisdom is expressed to take more seriously than we often do the possibility that a marital partner found something that he or she needed when marrying his/her particular spouse. "Impossible" marriages are often experienced as such because the persons in them have lost touch with the deeper self that responded to what they needed in the other person. Much of what is done in the pastoral counseling of couples is helping each person get in touch with that deeper self. Probably the worst mistake a pastoral counselor can make in response to a marriage is to make a quick judgment, based on present behavior, that this is a "bad" marriage. Much more is going on than he or she can possibly understand; therefore, judgments about the quality of a marriage are best left to someone else. The pastoral counselor should be too busy trying to understand individuals and how they function together to draw any conclusions about the outcome of the marital conflict.

Although we have used the concept of covenant and the biblical image of the individual in community to deepen our understanding of marriage and family relationships, conventional wisdom derived from other relationships does not apply in any simple form to marriage. "All's fair in love and war and marriage is both" is John Warkentin's way of putting it. There is a potential depth of sharing and intimacy in marriage which can inform other relationships, but in itself is unique. The practical implication of this is that the pastoral counselor needs to be careful in applying generalizations about relationships to a particular marriage. The task at hand is to see what is, what works, and what does not work, not to struggle with what *ought* to be. Because intimacy and depth of relationships are far more a feeling than a thinking dimension of life, it is not possible to learn enough or learn the right things in order to avoid pain in a marriage. Pain and brokenness are a normal part of the marriage relationship and cannot be avoided. They are human mysteries to be lived through. The commitment to intimacy which is central to marriage is in fact a commitment to live through the pain that closeness brings. One of the major functions of the pastoral counseling of married persons consists of finding ways to remind them of that reality.

Another practical implication of this understanding of marriage and the family is that a couple's move toward divorce can often be understood as a healthy need for distance and freedom which can also be found in a marriage as well as apart from it. Human intimacy needs are so great that pastoral counselors often experience couples more stuck together than estranged, expecting more from each other than it is possible for them to give. Counseling technique requires in effect pulling the couples apart and temporarily meeting some of their insatiable dependency needs in the counseling relationship. They can learn through a pastoral relationship to feed emotionally in relationships other than the marriage, so that the marriage can be unique, or at least adult—one that offers more meat than milk.

Pastoral Counseling Is Intergenerational

A marriage is an intragenerational relationship. To break the impasses of that relationship, the introduction of someone from another generation is needed. In order to see their deeper selves without the blinders of present-day pain, the couple needs to have the option of regressing to a situation in which they can be parented. The old phrase, "going home to mother," expresses an important need which can often be met more effectively in a pastoral counseling experience where the "mother" does not have an agenda of her own to work on. Because the nuclear family in our mobile society is so often cut off from adequate parenting, pastoral counseling with couples and families can usefully provide intergenerational, experiential learning. Pastoral counseling with couples is two-generational; with families, three-generational or more. An alternative to the extended intergenerational family of our forebears seems necessary for adequate emotional growth, particularly in times of stress.

Thus, the pastoral counselor often functions as parent or grandparent, and on occasion, son or daughter, in order to reduce the demandingness of a nuclear family's alliances and provide an experience of relational humanness. The counselor functions symbolically in the various roles relevant to the several members of the family in order that they may reestablish their own individual growth processes and learn to deal responsibly with their parenting generation.

The need to be parented is never fully satisfied, but the demands or claim on one's parent can be surrendered or dealt with more honestly than is usually the case in troubled families. Jacob can learn to stand before Isaac and ask for his blessing without having to pretend to be a "hairy man" rather than the "smooth man" he really is (Gen. 27:11 KJV). He is then free to become a parent along with Isaac and Abraham. Because we are all historical creatures, one could suggest symbolically that a primary goal of pastoral counseling with families is to enable the adults in a family to transcend their own generation—to come to terms with the prior one and learn to parent the one who follows them. For the children, the goal is to develop appropriately to their own stage in life without having to transcend their generation prematurely in response to unsatisfied parental need.

I resist the dogmatism that interprets literally the Genesis injunction to "be fruitful and multiply." Not every family should have children physically. There is, however, something important to be heard in the command to be fruitful. I have found in couples who have come for pastoral counseling a persistent need to create something that will transcend their own generation. A child is the biological response to the command to be creative, but there are other responses in which a couple can experience themselves as co-creators who extend beyond their own generation. Pastoral counseling must be alert to this apparent basic human need and assist a couple in fulfilling it.

What follows is the practical application of what has been said thus far in the work with couples. If the focus of the problem seems to be the pain of one or both of the marital partners in relation to functioning as an adult rather than as a parent, then the unit of care can be determined to be the couple. Although I believe that most of what has been said thus far is applicable to work with one, two, and three generation families, my perspective is limited by the fact that the great majority of my experience, both in giving and receiving care, has been with couples rather than entire families. Detailed development and illustration of the offering of relationship humanness to entire family systems must wait for further experience and theoretical reflection. I suggest only some brief implications for family work at the end of this chapter. I turn now to how my understanding of the way pastoral counseling of a couple involves both an intervention in the marital system and a pastoral relationship to each person. The terms used to describe the process, "system intervening" and "pastoral relating" are not mutually exclusive, but represent emphases on the systemic and the relational.

Stages in the Pastoral Counseling of Couples

SYSTEM INTERVENING	*PASTORAL RELATING*
1. Structuring to become involved in the marital system	1. Asserting pastoral responsibility for each person in the marriage
2. "In-betweening" or pulling partners apart	2. Pain-sharing with each person
3. Supervising relationship observation	3. Providing a pseudo-marriage or "in the room" affair
4. Consulting on marital communication	4. Giving pastoral blessing to the remarriage
5. Exciting the system	5. Learning to say good-bye

I discuss in some detail each of these five stages in the pastoral counseling of couples. The sequencing of the stages is not rigid in the sense that once stage three has been reached there is no longer any need for the emphases of stages one and two. As in human development, some kind of regression may occur at any stage in the process. However, the regression more often than not is not a defeat but a necessary part of the process of moving forward. Getting hung up on a later stage and trying to deal with the situation without going back to what was called for earlier is a greater problem than going back to an earlier stage in the process. For example, the most common error that I make in counseling couples is allowing myself to believe that a couple is ready for consultation on their communication when active intervention is still called for.

Stage One: Structuring to become involved in the marital system and establishing pastoral relationships. I have previously discussed the structuring of the counseling process from the point of view of its value in creating optimum conditions for the work. Structuring, within the context of this chapter, may be seen as both an intervention into the marital system and an assertion of pastoral responsibility to relate to both persons in the marriage. In the telephone conversation with Joyce Osment discussed earlier, rather than simply accepting Mrs. Osment's statement that she does not need to talk to her husband because she already knows what he will say, the pastor insists that she do it anyway.

Pastoral
Counselor: I know that you probably do know what he'll say, but try it anyway. Tell him that it's just my way of doing things, and maybe he will understand. Call me back tomorrow and tell me what he said.

In this statement, the pastoral counselor has made an active intervention into the marital system. He has avoided arguing about what the husband will do. He has no experience to contradict the wife's authority on that. Rather, he creates a new circumstance in the marriage and asks the husband to respond to the pastoral counselor's interaction with his wife. He is saying, in effect, "This is not the same as before. See if it's not different with me involved in the situation." Through this telephone interaction, before the counseling actually begins, the pastor has created a triangle that can upset the marital balance in a potentially creative way.[8] The intervention sets up the situation that will be taking place in the early stages of the counseling—one partner (in this case, the husband) being challenged to respond to the interaction of the other two.

In addition to its function as system intervention and pattern-breaking, however, the pastoral counselor's attempt to structure the situation is also an assertion of pastoral responsibility. It does not follow that because an individual asks for help that the best way to offer help is individually. The picture of God's relationship to individuals in community can be a guiding one for pastoral role. In asking a potential counselee that her spouse be involved, the pastor is saying, "It is important for me to be personally related to those who are most important to you." Good pastoral counseling offers a powerful relationship that can demonstrate the relational quality of a marriage. The pastoral calling is to be related as significantly as possible to each member of a marital system.

Another way of thinking about both dimensions of stage one is through the image of the affair. Intervention into the marital system and insistence on relationship to both persons in the marriage can be seen as a way of having a non-secretive affair. It involves bringing into the marriage a dimension that was absent, or severely needed, under conditions that respect the marital commitment rather than substituting for it. A pastoral counselor who passively or without reflection enters a long-term counseling relationship with one member of a marriage may in effect, without any physical contact, be having a secretive affair that can be ultimately destructive to the marriage. Pastoral counseling with both members of the couple present can meet some of the personal needs addressed by an affair, but do so openly, so that the marriage is strengthened rather than undermined. It is a useful but temporary triangle which allows both members of the couple to satisfy emotional needs and achieve insights into the way relationships can work. More of this can be seen in the next stage.

Stage Two: "In-betweening" and pain-sharing. Stage two marks the most difficult part of the pastoral counseling of couples, certainly the most exhausting. I am following a course, already set in stage one, that emphasizes aggressive intervention into what is presently going on in the marriage and insisting on relationship to each person in spite of their efforts to leave the counselor out. Early in a counseling relationship a couple will consistently resist the pastoral counselor's efforts to intervene and become related to each of them by clinging to their old and painful ways of relating to each other.

Although the strength of this resistance will vary according to the emotional need of each member of the couple, there is in every couple a kind of bilateral transference that seeks in this relationship that which was not satisfactorily dealt with in relationships with the family of origin. (See definition and discussion of transference in chapter 7.) Because the marital partner is not primarily organized to meet the spouse's needs but only to meet his or her own, the effort is at least partially frustrated. The partners become locked together in their frustration somewhat like boxers in a clinch, expecting more from the relationship than it can possibly supply.

The words from Gibran's *The Prophet* are continually instructive: "Let there be spaces in your togetherness."[9] I often find myself saying to a couple that most of those who come to me for counseling are really asking me to help them get farther apart instead of closer together. The exceptions to this are the couples who have already panicked over their unsatisfactory dependence on each other and have physically separated, had an affair, or filed for divorce. The task with such couples differs in that it involves encouraging them to stay close enough together to see what happens while they decide whether dissolving the relationship is more of a rational choice than an emotional reaction.

Actually, the evaluation process to be discussed in chapter 6 is a valuable aid for coming in between them and for developing a pastoral relationship to each one. Without a structure for the pastoral counselor to follow in conducting the early interviews virtually nothing happens except the pastor's observing repetition of the marital argument and frustration. I disagree strongly with the literature on marriage counseling that suggests that the counselor should spend a significant amount of time early in the counseling process observing the marital interaction in order that he/she can interpret the pathology in the communication and suggest improvements.[10] In my experience this is almost inevitably premature. Before this type of interaction can be effective, the couple needs the stabilizing and sustaining effect of a sigificant relationship to the pastoral counselor. The stability of the two relationships, one to each member of the couple, can have the effect of two feet firmly planted on the ground. When that has been done a variety of techniques can be used to improve marital communication. When it has not been done, most of the interpretative work related to the marriage will have to be done over again.

The structure for evaluating the human situation of each member of the couple and the marriage is intended to contribute to an understanding of that situation and to develop pastoral relationships to each person. The initial focus on the pain in the situation as each person experiences it is an attempt to move as quickly as possible to the affective dimension in each person's life. It is also a way to move toward a pastoral relationship through sharing the pain each person experiences in his or her situation. With some persons, this is almost immediately. With others, the task of the pastoral counselor is to teach the person how to participate in such a relationship and begin to use it.

I have used the terms, "aggressive intervention," "pulling apart," "in-betweening," and the like to describe the pastoral style of responding to the couple at this stage in the counseling process. I would like to remind the relatively inexperienced pastor, who thinks these terms describe a style too far removed from what he or she feels able to do, that I am attempting to present the old and familiar rather than the strange and new. However aggressive or knowledgeable about marriage and family dynamics a pastor may be, his style of intervention, which I am describing, may be thought of as asserting the ancient prerogative of establishing a pastoral relationship with all those in his/her charge. Those who come for help have, in effect, joined that group of persons for whom the pastoral counselor has responsibility.

What should be done at this stage in the counseling process is essentially the same as what a pastor does in a traumatic grief situation where there is much emotionality, chaos, and confusion. He or she moves into the chaos to structure a relationship to the principal parties in the grief, attempting to shut out the other things that are going on and insisting on relationship to those in most need. This can be a paradigm for marital and family intervention. The pastor's thoughts at such a time might be something like this: *I must break into this conversation in order to establish a relationship with each person here.* In doing this I am involved in an old and familiar task of pastoral work, ignoring the chaos that may be present and doing my best to relate to persons who are hurting.

In the case of Bob and Betty, the pastoral method of evaluation and relationship building attempted to provide a strong counterpoint to the pain and stuckness that they felt with each other.

Pastoral
Counselor: *(To Bob)* Can you tell me what's hurting in your life situation, how whatever's going on is affecting you?

> **Bob:** Let me tell you how it all started. Betty has never been able to give up her mother. That's what broke up her first marriage and when we—
>
> **P.C.:** Wait just a minute. I think you misunderstood me. I want to hear the story, but I need to hear first how it's affecting you. How do you feel? How is the whole thing getting to you now? What's it like for you?
>
> **Bob:** Well, I just thought you needed to know about that.
>
> **P.C.:** I do, but it's more important to know your feelings now. I'm not sure if you feel sad, angry, confused, or what it is you're feeling.
>
> **Bob:** I don't know. I think a little of all of that. It feels kind of hopeless to me.

That brief interaction is an illustration of "in-betweening" and the beginning of pain-sharing. Bob's pain is more important than the information he wants to give. Actually, getting to the "facts of the case" is a way of avoiding the pain. The pastoral counselor's task is to remind Bob that sharing his pain and other intense feelings is what marriage is all about. The pastor gets "in-between" Bob and Betty by insisting that Bob talk about what is going on with him rather than blaming Betty for the situation. The pastor is quite aggressive in his intervention. He does it quietly and calmly, but he simply does not allow Bob to say what he had intended to say. He does not argue, assumes that Bob will do what needs to be done if he understands what is of first importance, and then goes back to his question, this time phrased somewhat differently.

Bob becomes a bit defensive and attempts to justify the way he had started out. This assures him of the pastor's interest but changes the priorities. Many times it is simply not possible to move toward feelings as quickly as this illustration suggests. Bob may be so "programmed" that he must do some of it his way. The important thing is for the pastor to stick to his goal and keep coming back to it, pushing Bob to share his feelings about his situation. At the point Bob begins to share his feelings, the pastoral relationship is being developed, an initial trust is established, and "one foot" is planted firmly enough for Bob to talk about his hopelessness without being overcome by it.

As long as the pastoral counselor moves to establish the priority of pain-sharing, a great deal of time can be spent in getting acquainted with the couple's life situation along the lines to be suggested in the following chapter. In getting the story, however, it is important for the pastor to make it clear that what he/she is hearing is each person's way of seeing the situation, telling the story, and sharing feelings about it rather than trying to get the "facts" of the case. I often say to couples, "I'm really not interested in the truth. What is important right now is how each of you sees and experiences the situation. That's what we can work with." In the process of hearing the story the pastor structures the situation to hear from each one in turn, minimizing interruptions and corrections from the other. In the process of the evaluation, he/she attempts to become related to each person's story and feelings, avoiding insofar as possible, becoming entangled in the chaos or stuckness of the present situation.

At this stage in the process of pastoral counseling with a couple, marital fights are generally unproductive and should be broken up, if necessary, by sitting literally in between the couple and having them relate only to the pastor rather than to each other. Learning to fight effectively is an important part of marriage, but it cannot be done until there is stability in the relationship and until the pastoral relationships with each person have been firmly established. I often have to say to a couple as I come in between them, "Look. You already know how to fight this way. You're wasting your time and mine doing it with me. I want you to learn how to do something new." Or, "I have no interest in trying to tell you how to lead your life outside this room, but if you use anything that you heard said during our time together to hurt the other person when you are at home, you are undercutting what we are about here."

Once an evaluation is complete, the process of counseling at this stage consists of the pastoral counselor relating individually to each person in response to that person's present feelings and continuing life story. If at all possible this is done with both persons present so that the one not directly involved can learn from the way the pastor and his/her spouse are sharing feelings and story. The primary justification for seeing marital partners separately is when the pastor is unable to break up the fight or when either he/she is too weak, or the chaos too strong, to intervene successfully with both persons present. Seeing marital partners separately tends to slow down the counseling process because neither partner has the opportunity to learn from the other person's relationship to the pastor.

When the partners can be seen together, the interaction might go something like this part of the relationship with Bob and Betty:

> **Bob:** The whole thing is like this. When she gets with her mother, she acts like it's like it was when she was a little girl. She thinks she doesn't have to worry about money. She and her mother just do anything they want to do. She never asks me. *(He goes on at some length).*
>
> **P.C.:** Bob! You're talking about *them* again. What about you? What are you feeling when you tell me about that? It sounds like you feel helpless or out of control or something.
>
> **Bob:** Exactly! There's not a damn thing I can do about it. Why they—
>
> **P.C.:** Not they. You. The feelings you're having. What are they like?
>
> **Bob:** *(He goes back to his helpless, hopeless feeling and how it reminds him of what it was like when he was a child.)*
>
> **P.C.:** *(After listening and responding to Bob's feelings for some time, he turns to Betty.)* And what was going on in you while Bob and I were talking to each other?
>
> **Betty:** I was wishing that I knew how to make him stop like you did. With me he just goes on and on, and I feel frightened and don't know what to do. I pull back away from all of it, and that just makes him madder.

The pastoral counselor's first task is breaking into Bob's compulsive pattern of talking about things and attempting to help him focus on his feelings. As Bob talks about Betty and her mother (out there, in contrast to within himself) it seems that there is no relationship between him and anyone else. One can feel his isolation even in the brief comments given here. He is the part of the triangle that is left out when the mother and daughter become a couple.

Part of the intervention is the refocusing of his communication on what he is feeling rather than what others are doing. The counselor attempts to break up the telling of the same old story. Equally important, however, is his pulling Bob into a relationship with him. Instead of a triangle, Bob, Betty, and the mother-in-law, in which Bob is excluded, there is a new triangle, Bob, Betty and the pastoral counselor, in which Bob is included. The pastor insists that Bob talk to him about his feelings instead of just talking. He experiences his feelings in relationship instead of denying them by talking about what's wrong with Betty and her mother.

Although at first Betty is left out of this new triangle, she soon becomes a part of it when the pastor moves to her and attempts to get in touch with her feelings. Bob is left out, but it is a conscious and intentional leaving out in order to be let in. The pattern of couple formation within a triangle, which is characteristic of life, is used intentionally, but used in a way that allows the person left out to participate by observing what is going on and using that as a stimulus to reflect on his or her own feelings. This beginning movement back and forth between the couples within the triangle signals the beginning of stage three in the pastoral counseling process.

There is no sharp completion of the work of stage two in the move to stage three. The two stages appear together for much of the counseling process with the necessity of pulling partners apart and moving in between gradually, giving way to more of a supervisory than a direct intervention process. If the move is more into stage three than stage two, it indicates that the pastoral relationships have been established and that the marital pain is less threatening because both relational "feet" have been firmly planted. The pastoral relationship is usually stronger with one member of the couple than with the other. This presents no particular problem as long as the pastoral counselor continues to work to develop a stronger relationship with the less-involved member of the couple. The relative strength of the relationships may vary as the process moves along.

Stage Three: Supervising relationship observation and providing a pseudo-marriage. Getting to stage three in the process of the pastoral counseling of couples is like getting to a plateau on a mountain climb. There will be other strenuous parts of the climb, but shorter ones, followed by more plateaus and opportunities to enjoy the view. As I have suggested earlier, the major satisfaction in pastoral counseling comes from being in relationship. The structuring and intervening is done primarily to make relationship possible. Certainly, it has other benefits, such as helping couples and families discover that there are alternative ways of thinking about and experiencing things. From a pastoral point of view, as we have attempted to describe it, growth and change take place primarily through the power of a caring relationship.

In stage three, the pastoral counselor is related, not equally, but significantly to each member of the couple. The process of counseling involves the satisfactory experiencing of those relationships by each partner while the other partner observes and attempts to learn from what is going on. A pseudo-marriage is created between the pastor and, insofar as possible, each member of the couple, or one might think of the relationship as an affair, but not a secret affair. It is an affair that takes place "in the room," so that the couple may learn from what it offers.

The pastoral relationships in counseling with couples are like a marriage in that they offer the kind of caring and sharing that is a central feature of a satisfactory marriage. It is the feature that is most obviously absent in a troubled marriage.

The counselee who is in such a relationship is not learning just about his or her marriage, but is experiencing what much of the emotional dimension of marriage is like—being respected, valued, and understood by another person. What has not been going on, or not going on effectively, between the marriage partners is now occurring between the counselee and the pastor. It is not particularly important to identify how much of this is "real" and how much is transference. The important thing is that the pastoral relationship offers a temporary emotional feeding which takes some of the demand and frustration off of the actual marital relationship.

It is a *pseudo-marriage,* not a real one, and for a number of reasons. By intent it is temporary, like an affair, and designed to fill an immediate need. Perhaps more significant, it is "pseudo" because it is intergenerational and more like a parent-child relationship than a peer relationship. Although the counselor and counselee may be the same age, the pastoral counseling situation is structured so that it can never be fully reciprocal. (The helping person is inevitably placed in a parental role. This assumes that a marriage should be a relationship that can be fully reciprocal and equal.) Because of this, the goal of the relationship is not permanence and continued growth, as in a real marriage, but one of sufficient need satisfaction, so that the relationship will, like a parental one, gradually become less necessary.

Bob: *(At the beginning of the seventh or eighth interview)* I've been writing down things that I particularly wanted you to understand. *(Looks at his notes)* I don't think you know just how easy it is for me to feel rejected. I'll be feeling great, have a positive attitude about selling, have four prospects lined up for the day, and my boss can make me feel rejection just by acting busy. It's the same way with Betty. If she doesn't pay any attention to me, I'll feel down and try and change it, and the more I try to make her change, the more she seems to ignore me. *(Bob goes on and on, and after awhile the counselor turns to Betty.)*

127

P.C.: What do you see going on between Bob and me?

Betty: You looked interested for awhile, and then you looked bored.

P.C.: I was getting bored. Does that ever happen to you?

Betty: *(Laughs)* It sure does, but I don't want to make him feel bad, so I try to listen.

P.C.: I was about to tell him that I had stopped listening, but I thought maybe you had been there too.

Betty: I still have trouble stopping him. If I could learn to do that without hurting his feelings, but Bob's so sensitive.

P.C.: Maybe if you let him know when you've stopped listening, he'll understand that you're just not able to take it all in without a break. You could be interrupting because you care about what he's saying rather than you don't care. I think that's the reason I did it. I like Bob too much to feel good about getting bored with him.

In this section of the interview, the pastoral counselor listened as well as he could about Bob's feelings of rejection, sensing that there was really no way that he could avoid being perceived as rejecting Bob himself. Bob was reacting both to the present situation and to the experience in relationships that he had brought in from the past. There were several choices that the pastor could have made in responding to Bob. The poorest of these would have been for him to act as if he were listening after he had stopped. He might have told Bob directly what he was experiencing in the relationship with him. He chose, however, to get at the same issue by bringing in Betty and trying to relate his dialogue with Bob to Betty's experience, which he assumed would in some way be parallel. He and Betty talked openly in Bob's presence about what it was like being related to Bob. The pastor's assumption was that Bob could learn more about himself and the way others experience him by hearing himself talked about than by being talked to. In the process, he was also responding to Betty's feelings while Bob observed it. And finally—although there is much more going on than I can discuss here—he modeled different ways to be in relationship to both Bob and Betty so each could learn from them. He was being in relationship and supervising the couple in observing and learning from relationships.

I have described this stage in the counseling process as less exhausting and more satisfying. Correspondingly, the interventions into the marital system at this point seem less aggressive than in stages one and two. It is, however, intervention, in that the relational process, whenever it is going on, is stopped and redirected. The less-involved person in the triangle is challenged to respond to what is going on. The movement of the counseling is not just in one relationship, but optimally, in both. The primary elements in the process are the satisfaction of being in relationship and the observation and learning from other significant persons in relationship. It is like supervision because the pastoral counselor has a perspective on what is going on and can use it to point out some things that the counselees cannot see. The task being supervised is the observing and learning from relationship.

Betty: *(Later in the session)* I get so frightened when he really gets angry. Usually he just gets disgusted with me when I don't respond and goes away, but when he's angry I feel like it used to be when my father was drunk and shouting in the next room. *(She cries for awhile.)*

P.C.: What other feelings are in those tears, Betty? Can you put any of them into words?

Betty: I don't know.

P.C.: I know you don't know for sure, but try anyway. You have some sense of what the feelings are like.

Betty: Like being completely helpless. Not knowing whether I'm going to be hurt or be living in the same house tomorrow or have anyone to take care of me. *(Silence except for tears)*

P.C.: *(After some time)* Being cared for when you're frightened is one of the things I think you feel here with

129

> me. You must have gotten the idea that that was
> something you couldn't have. *(Pause)* I hope you can
> enjoy it. *(Another long pause while Betty cries a bit
> more)*

P.C.: *(To Bob)* Do you know what you were feeling then?

Bob: I'm not sure. I felt bad that she was crying and wished I
knew something to do about it.

P.C.: What did I do about it?

Bob: You mostly let her cry.

Again, there is a great deal more going on in this part of the
session than can be discussed here. Perhaps the most
important thing is the experiencing of some relational
humanness, of honesty, of being cared for, and the treating of
all this as if it were a normal and important part of life, not a
problem to be solved. The pastoral counselor attempts to
respond to Betty's pain in a way that not only offers real
satisfaction, but also gives Bob an opportunity to observe and
re-experience what relationship is all about. Both Bob and
Betty have been so caught up in their own needs and the
frustration of them that they have had limited experience in
responding successfully to each other. The process of
counseling at this point is intended to open up that possibility.

**Stage Four: Consulting on marital communication and
blessing the remarriage.** A good portion of the couples whom I
see in pastoral counseling never get to this stage in the process.
What they need is the part of the counseling that helps break
up the trap of frustrated expectations and focuses on
rediscovering one's individuality. Once they discover some
freedom from each other they become freer to choose each
other and therefore do not need a third person to help them
decide what to do together. Probably the most common
reason any kind of counseling terminates is because the
concerns outside the counseling relationship become more
pressing than those inside. When the members of a couple
rediscover some of their individuality and freedom, this very

often takes place. To some extent, then, stages four and five may be seen as optional at extra cost. The central issues in the pastoral counseling of couples and families are getting unstuck, experiencing oneself as free while with one's partner, and re-experiencing some of the feeding and reparenting that can best come from a member of a different generation, such as a pastor. Individually, it involves dealing with one's own sin. And this needs to take place to a significant degree before "marriage counseling" can begin, or, at least, before it can be very effective.

What I mean by "marriage counseling" in this context is, literally, counseling on the marriage. This most often means working on communication skills, but, potentially, it may involve any number of issues that come up in a couple's life together: money management, in-laws, sex, parenting. The valuable literature that has been written about these important issues can assist the pastoral counselor and the couple in dealing with them.[11] The major problem is that it is these issues that are often addressed and not the more fundamental ones that we have attempted to deal with in stages one through three. It is not uncommon for me to see in my ministry of pastoral counseling a couple who has been through a program of marriage enrichment or education.[12] Most frequently they will say, "That was good, and it helped for awhile, but it wasn't enough, or it ran out, or it made us realize how bad things really were." It is difficult to deal effectively with marital concerns without bringing up the central issues of human pain and brokenness, the deviousness of our sin, and the desperate need for a caring relationship. This is why ministers cannot afford to lose touch with pastoral counseling in their efforts to do "marriage counseling."

Another reason to maintain this perspective is the importance of a pastor's ministry to those who do not choose to continue their marriage. Stages one through three in the pastoral counseling of couples address issues that must be dealt with regardless of whether or not a couple stays together. They can be addressed in individual counseling, but they can be more adequately confronted by the couple together as they actually see what doesn't work and check it out with a third person, rather than maintaining their unrealistic fantasies about the relationship. If pastors understand their work with couples primarily as counseling about a marriage and the marriage does not continue, they usually look on the counseling as a failure. I am convinced that some of my best work with couples has been done with persons whose marriages did not continue. Their referral to me of other persons suggest that many of them agree.

If the relationship to the couple in counseling develops into stage four, the system intervention side of the process can best be described as consultation. It is an intervention, in that the pastoral counselor stops what is going on in the relationship with the couple and comments on it, but the style of intervention is very different from previous stages. It is *consultative* in the sense that we have used this word before. The responsibility for the relationship rests with the couple. The counselor interprets what he or she sees them doing with it and then backs away, leaving the couple to continue what they are doing in the relationship. The pastoral counselor can recognize when this stage has begun when the couple consistently does some things right in their communication with each other.

Quite often I see this in the waiting room before a couple comes in for their appointment. Rather than sitting in stony silence, looking anxious about at the other persons there, they seem to be planning something. They may be disagreeing, but they keep on the same issue in spite of it. They seem almost reluctant to come into my office when I indicate that I am ready to see them. I sit in silence after they are seated in the office and watch what goes on. They may occasionally look over at me, but they seem more concerned with each other than with me. After awhile I may comment:

> **P.C.:** You're doing pretty well. It's fun to watch you.
> **Betty:** What do you mean?

P.C.: Whatever you're working on you seem to be at it together, and I remember times not too long ago when I could not imagine this happening.

Bob: It feels good to me too. Betty listens to me now.

P.C.: Now that you don't need her to listen as much as you once did.

Bob: I don't know about that, but I like it.

P.C.: One of the things I noticed that didn't seem to work as well as the rest was when you said—*(The counselor comments on a particular part of the communication).* It looked like Betty may have turned you off at that point. *(Turning to Betty)* Do you remember what you were feeling then?

Betty: *(Responds to the question)* A little irritated, I think.

P.C.: I think when you become aware of feeling this sort of thing that it would be good to interrupt Bob to tell him so and why, if you know, and then go back to the subject at hand. Remember the part in the Satir book[13] about . . .

A consultative intervention goes on something like that with some interpretation and some teaching. Then the couple moves back to talk to each other without any instruction to do so. The experience of the pastoral counselor at this point is something like Henry Higgins' in *My Fair Lady,* after the long process of teaching Eliza how to talk: "She's got it! I think she's got it!" They've got it! Or at least they've got enough of it to do it themselves rather than have the counseling relationship focus primarily between each of them and the pastoral counselor. Many things can go on at this stage, some of them quite intense. The issues discussed may range over the whole spectrum of marriage relationship. Sometimes there is regression back to stage three and the need for a more direct, emotionally feeding relationship to the counselor. Once this stage is reached, however, most of the strong, aggressive intervention is over and the consultative mode prevails.

On the side of pastoral relating, what happens can best be described as blessing, supporting, or confirming. The movement is not unlike that of a traditional marriage service. The couple speak to the minister in their first interaction in the service, the "wilt thou's." They move to interaction with each other, coached by the minister, the making of vows to each other, and the giving of rings. Then, they receive a blessing. In this stage of the counseling process, the couple has demonstrated a renewed abilty to interact constructively with each other, and that interaction is blessed by the pastoral counselor. They have, in effect, engaged in the process of remarrying.

Stage Five: Exiting the system and learning to say good-bye. The final stage of the process in terms of system intervention is moving out altogether. The couple carries on their own relationship, and the pastoral counselor watches from outside. In terms of pastoral relating, good-byes are said. Sometimes, on the relationship side, "good-bying" may take some time. Usually, this occurs when there have been important unresolved issues with real parents. Individual counseling with one member of the couple may be appropriate at this point, if possible, with the spouse coming into the sessions as often as possible in order to stay in touch with the important emotional issues in his mate's life. In any case, dealing with good-bye in pastoral counseling is an important part of the completing past grief work and preparing oneself to face the inevitable losses in life with some grace and sense of purpose.

In addressing the question of the unit of care in pastoral counseling, I have, in this chapter, presented the point of view that the pastoral counseling of couples and families is of a piece with the pastoral counseling of individuals. It is not some other skill that pastors learn to do, but a broadening of the pastoral care they do with individuals to include marital and family systems. Whatever the unit of care, the relationship to individual persons remains fundamental. It is, in fact, the means by which a pastor intervenes into a locked-together family system. Relational humanness is offered to each member of the system. To the extent that the offering of relationship and the intervention into the present unsatisfactory pattern of marital and family relationships is effective is dealing with the problems of human pain and brokenness, it becomes possible to consult with and counsel the marriage or family. Attempting to do this before the deeper issues of the human situation have been addressed is premature and often ineffective. It tends to identify the success of pastoral counseling with couples with "saving the marriage," whereas the responsibility of the pastor is not to save but to offer relational humanness in the midst of the pain of life and relationships.

Short-Term Family Intervention

Both in parishes and in pastoral counseling centers there seem to be more opportunities to work extensively with couples than to work with whole families. On the other hand, particularly in the parish, there is a significant opportunity for relatively short-term family intervention and care. In this kind of ministry, it is essential that the pastor assert his/her responsibility for and interest in the whole family and for each member of the family. Although an adequate exploration of the implications of the view of pastoral counseling presented here for work with entire families is beyond the scope of this chapter and of my present experience, I believe that most of the principles stated earlier in relation to couples also apply to the pastor's relationship to a family.

Briefly stated, some additional principles may be useful in assisting the pastor to extend his or her ministry to a larger unit of care.

1. Whatever their level of training in family therapy, the pastor can use what they already know (something about the pastoral care of persons) to intervene in a family system.

2. Whatever is done, however, must be done actively and aggressively if it is to have any significant impact on the family system or on the individuals while they are in that system. For

a relatively passive minister, working with families requires learning to change his or her basic style of relationship.

3. The pastor should bring all the family together, but talk to them individually, insisting that each one talk to him/her rather than continuing the existing pattern of relationships.

4. As in all pastoral counseling, the pastor should look for feelings and respond to pain, but not ignore the other members of the family in doing so.

5. The pastor is an outsider to the family system and will continually feel this, but he or she can be an insider to each of the individuals within the system.

6. The purpose of pastoral counseling with families, whatever the presenting problem, is to offer relational humanness to each member of the family in a way that will enable family members to change the balance and boundaries that bind them to rigid roles and functions. Significant relationship to the intervening pastor can enable persons within the system to see and act on choices open to them that they had not seen before.

These principles are intended to be more suggestive than dogmatic.[14] Pastors must develop their own style. The major qualifier to this, however, is that if the unit of care for pastoral counseling is the family, the pastor's style needs to be active, intervening, and relational with all members of the system.

I turn now to the problem of defining the human situation to which pastoral counseling is addressed.

Chapter Six

What Hurts?—Diagnosis in Pastoral Counseling

This chapter is about diagnosis and its value for the pastoral counselor. That being said, it is important to indicate rather quickly what I do not plan to do. I will not be dealing directly with those categories of psychiatric diagnosis, familiar to all who have worked in a mental health setting.[1] My purpose, instead, is to consider, from a pastoral point of view, the question raised by the Menninger Foundation symposium edited by Paul Pruyser, *Diagnosis and the Difference It Makes* and developed for pastors in *The Minister as Diagnostician.*[2] In contrast to Pruyser, I will be speaking from within the profession of ministry, without his additional agenda of helping clergy with their feelings of inadequacy. My task is simply to remind my colleagues in ministry of the pastoral counseling movement's contribution to answering the question, What's going on with this person who has asked for help?

For the pastor who is not a specialist in pastoral counseling, the position taken here is that useful diagnostic skill can be achieved without a detailed knowledge of the language of mental health. For the specialist, who must know how to use mental health language effectively, the chapter may serve as a reminder to the pastoral counselor that mental health language is not enough. Something more needs to be understood and used in the pastoral relationship. The specialist in pastoral counseling must be the master of at least two languages because he or she may be working in a setting where mental health language is the primary mode of discourse. Even in such as setting, however, it is more important for the pastoral counselor to be concerned with the deeper issues of what it means to be human, as this is understood Christianly, than to be able to classify persons with the appropriate diagnostic category.

In his novel, *The Last Gentleman,* Walker Percy points to what is, perhaps, the central problem of diagnosis, "How does knowledge about the human situation contribute to living in or changing that situation?"

> His trouble is he wants to know what his trouble is. His "trouble" he thinks, is a disorder of such a character that if only he can locate the right expert with the right psychology, the disorder can be set right . . . his posture is self-defeating.[3]

Certain knowledge may obstruct change rather than contribute to it. It may reinforce the passive dependency potential of the helping situation by solidifying the roles of "doctor" and "patient" in a way that undercuts the counselee's responsibility for his or her life situation.

The quotation also points to the human tendency to objectify and externalize one's "problem." The point of view of this chapter, in contrast, is that knowledge of a particular human situation (diagnostic knowledge) contributes in three ways to living in and changing that situation: (1) the dialogical process of securing such knowledge facilitates the building of relationship through the sharing of a person's story, feelings, and hopes; (2) it contributes to a person's *owning* his or her story, seeing the "problem" as internal as well as external, and taking more responsibility for his/her life; and (3) the diagnostic process aids in the discovery and acceptance of what is common and what is unique in one's human situation, thus beginning to identify what can and what cannot be changed.

This preliminary statement of the contributions of the diagnostic process has revealed two important assumptions about that process which will continue to be evident as the discussion proceeds. First, it is a process, an increasingly accurate or useful way of describing what is going on with a person. It is not simply an identification of a person as this or that. Second, it is dialogical, a task of both counselor and counselee, as they attempt to develop a common language about the counselee's human situation. It is not simply a judgment arrived at by the pastoral counselor in order to determine what treatment to apply in the case.

The Diagnostic Use of the "Magic Questions"

I begin the discussion of these issues by returning to the "magic questions" of chapter 4, noting now how they function in clarifying the human situation to which pastoral counseling is addressed. The tasks of relationship building, encouraging responsibility, and the discovery of what is common and what is unique will be evident throughout. The chapter concludes with an outline of a diagnostic interview conducted according to these principles and assumptions and an example of the kind of diagnostic feedback that might be given to counselees.

The question, What do you want? or What are you looking for? makes an important assumption about the person seeking help, namely, that he or she is actively seeking change and is taking some responsibility to see that change occurs. If one takes this assumption seriously, another assumption is attached to it—the counselee has the capacity to change what needs to be changed about himself or herself. One of the things I have heard consistently from counselees who have returned after the first diagnostic interview and have been asked for their reflections on the first session together is, "You acted as if there was hope for me." Or, even more positively stated, "You acted as if we could do something about our situation." The important words here are "acted as if," not anything stated by the pastoral counselor. He or she acted as if the counselee was a responsible human being, even though the counselee may not have acted very much like one.

The nature of the helping relationship is not, "Take care of me!" with the angry dependency implied in that demand. It is, rather, "I am going after something important, and I would like you to assist me in that enterprise." Acting toward the counselee according to these assumptions strongly affects the way the counseling proceeds as well as affecting the image of humankind which the pastoral counselor and counselee are working on together. Thus, dignity and potential maturity are perceived in the counselee, in spite of the sin and brokenness which may be a part of his or her life.

An illustration of this, which was important for me, occurred a number of years ago. I had two interviews with a young woman to whom "everything had happened that could possibily happen" to a person. That assessment, which I remember quite vividly, obviously grew out of my feelings of helplessness and inadequacy in the face of her mammoth problems. I could not imagine what I could possibly do for such a difficult counselee, so I told her that I needed to call in a consultant. (I believe that it is important in any counseling situation to pave the way for the option of consultation. One's counselees should know at the outset that the pastor may need to ask for help. I believe that more inadequate or dangerous counseling is done when a counselor is attempting to prove his or her adequacy and self-sufficiency than at any other time.)

My consultant, another pastoral counselor, listened for awhile to the string of "impossible" problems faced by my counselee and then abruptly asked her, pointing first to me and then to himself, "Do you like him better or me?" Stopping in mid-problem and after some hesitation, she said, "Well I suppose I like him (pointing to me) better. I've known him longer." "Oh," said my consultant with mock surprise, "you do make choices after all. I notice that you are sitting on the chair rather than on the couch. Do you like it better?" With some puzzlement, she answered that question and a series of similarly concrete and specific questions about what her choices were. Then my colleague commented, "So many things have just happened to you that I was afraid that you had stopped making choices. It looks like you can choose after all. Maybe you will be able to get something here." At this point then he asked her the magic question, which I, in worrying about my own inadequacy in the face of all those problems, had managed to forget. "What were you looking for in coming to the pastoral counseling service?" We were back on track again rather than being overcome by a series of impossible problems.

I do not present that illustration as a recommended technique for all pastoral counselors to follow. It grew out of the style of my consultant and is not applicable to all. My concern is to show through the illustration how the counseling has been structured and reduced to more manageable limits and to demonstrate how the pastoral counselor and counselee have participated together in making what is essentially a diagnostic judgment. It is assumed that the counselee is able to do something about her intolerable life situation. She is not simply asking that her pain be taken away, although she still may feel the latter concern quite strongly. She has chosen, with the support of the counselor, to do something about herself and her life. I am not suggesting that this is a simple, one-step process. The dialectic of the counseling will move back and forth between "I am choosing to do something about me" and "Damnit, why don't you take better care of me? This hurts too much." The process is facilitated by the other questions and their answers.

The second question, Why now? gets at the important assumption that "something has already changed in order to enable you to ask for help now. If some things can change, others can also change." The pastoral counselor cannot simply explain this assumption. Explanations are too easily contradicted by other explanations more familiar to the counselee. The assumptions need to be lived, just as in the worshiping church holy communion is celebrated, not only because it sometimes exists empirically in that community, but because the faith affirms that such communion is possible.

I discuss more of this affirming process in pastoral counseling in the chapters that follow. My interest here is in pointing out that, diagnostically, a person who can work on the Why now? question seems capable to deal with the fact that within much of the pain there is the potential for growth and change. One who cannot deal with the question except in terms of external reality—"he did something to me," or "something happened" has less potential for change.

The question, Why me? or Why this place? has diagnostic as well as structuring importance in knowing what kind of person or agency the counselee can identify with or receive help from. The greater the degree of choice and the more knowledge the counselee has about the person or agency to whom he or she is going for help, the more likelihood that help will be obtained.[4] This knowledge is important even when it is not the counselee's personal knowledge but the knowledge of a trusted referring person who takes care to fit him or her with an appropriate helper and place for help. An important part of the counselee's psychological strength is the ability to find and make use of the relationships which he or she needs. Formulating a picture of a person's abilities in this area is an important part of the diagnostic process.

I place the discussion of these questions first not because they must necessarily come first in a diagnostic interview, but because they are a reminder that they are the "high ground" of almost any interview. They are the points of view where the pastoral counselor can gain perspective on what is going on in the counseling situation. On occasion, for example, the woman "to whom everything had happened that could possibly happen," needs a consultant to lead her to that "high ground." In most cases just realizing that these questions provide such a point of view will be enough to keep the counselor from being overcome by the counselee's pain. I now turn to the diagnostic question of the degree to which persons seeking help locate the problem externally or internally to themselves.

External or Internal Location

Most persons who have consulted me during the years of my pastoral counseling practice first located their problem in some way external to themselves. Don Smith, in chapter 4, located the problem in what had happened to his son. Virtually every pastor can recall counseling sessions that began with the words, "My problem is my husband." Probably most persons who consult us are not naïve enough to locate the problem somewhere else without acknowledging some participation in it themselves. Initially, however, this is presented as a limited involvement. "Certainly I have some responsibility for what has happened, but not much. Most of the problem is out there or at least in the part of me that is not my real self."

Less frequently encountered, at least in my experience, are the persons who unrealistically see themselves as responsible for everything. Their inadequacy is so great that virtually every unfortunate thing that has happened to their families in the past five years is really their fault. They avoid analysis of the problem and, in effect, the possibility of change, by simplistically laying all blame on themselves. "My problem is out there" and "my problem is all me" are extreme ways of defining one's human situation which can mark two ends of a diagnostic continuum. The pastor's task in understanding the human situation to which his or her counseling is addressed is in making some judgment as to where on the continuum of external or internal problem definition the counselee is located. One of the pastor's primary goals in the counseling process is to assist the counselee to redefine the problem more realistically so that, following Reinhold Niebuhr's familiar words, he or she may change the things that can be changed, know the things that cannot be changed, and have the wisdom to know one from the other.

Christian Realism in Diagnosis

The development of "Christian realism" (a term sometimes used to designate Niebuhr's social philosophy) about the human situation of persons in pastoral counseling seems to me to be a norm to strive for. I have found Niebuhr's efforts to expose pretension of every sort helpful to me as I examine the way people avoid looking at the way things are with them. As useful as that norm is, however, it is important to recognize immediately that there is no one understanding of reality which the pastoral counselor is expected to be revealing—Christian or otherwise. The first words of Paul Horgan's novel, *Things as They Are,* suggest both the importance of the issue and the problem involved: " 'Richard, Richard,' they said to me in my childhood," when will you begin to see things as they are?' But they forgot that children are artists who see and enact through simplicity what their elders have lost through experience."[5]

The discovery and acceptance of "things as they are" needs to be qualified in at least one important way. Our reality is socially constructed. Adults as well as children are artists, although perhaps not creative ones.

> Man is biologically predestined to construct and to inhabit a world with others. This world becomes for him the dominant and definitive reality. Its limits are set by nature, but once constructed, this world acts back upon nature. In the dialectic between nature and the socially constructed world the human organism itself is transformed. In this same dialectic man produces reality and thereby produces himself.[6]

The reality that the diagnostic process begins to discover and discuss is the social construct of the counselee informed by his or her needs, values, and beliefs. The goal of the diagnostic process is increased awareness of that reality so that it may be intersected and affected by other views and interpretation of reality. The goal of the total counseling process is that these alternative views and interpretations of reality will affect feeling, thought, and action in ways that are useful to the counselees and the society around them. The process through which this ocurs will be discussed later. The diagnostic question that concerns us here is the degree to which the counselees' construction of reality involves them as actors within it rather than as passive onlookers.

Diagnostic Categories of the General Confession

Years ago, when I was a student at the University of Chicago Counseling Center, a group of us, representing several academic disciplines, reflected on our experience as beginning counselors. One of the students from the department of psychology, whom I had not thought of as particularly interested in religion, changed the direction of our discussion by asking me, "What is that prayer that you say in church which talks about having 'no health'?" I quoted for him some of the Prayer of General Confession: "We have left undone those things which we ought to have done; And we have done those things which we ought not to have done; And there is no health in us."[7] "That's it," he replied, "and I still don't like it—but it makes sense. The clients I have seen this year usually started off by telling me that they had this one problem, but if they stayed awhile, they usually ended up saying in some way or another, 'It's all of me that's the trouble.' The prayer bothers me, but it's true to my experience. There's not just one problem."

I suppose that the ambiguity of meaning conveyed by the phrase, "no health" may be the reason for omitting it from the present edition of *The Book of Common Prayer.*[8] Its omission, however, also omits some of the sounder theological and psychological wisdom about humankind. As much as I might wish it were the case, there is no simple location of most of the "problems" from which I suffer. They involve all of me, including my capacity for making decisions and taking responsibility.

The process of pastoral counseling can be understood as one in which the counselee gradually experiences the counseling relationship as one that offers enough security for him or her to acknowledge responsibility for the way things are. Only under such conditions can there be an experiential acknowledgment of "no health" to go along with the liturgical one. That no part of me is unaffected by the problem or that it is the *real* me that is at the heart of what's wrong is very close to the central Christian understanding of the human situation to which pastoral counseling and all ministry is addressed. The diagnostic question growing out of this is, To what degree does this person see himself or herself involved in the problem? What degree of responsibility for the situation does he or she affirm?

Much of what I have said thus far deals with the human situation common to us all. My concern now is to discuss how what is common relates to what is unique or, in terms of the Prayer of General Confession, how what we have done and not done relates to our "no health." How does the human situation express itself in this particular life or these lives?

Alice and Arthur are in their mid-thirties and their marriage is the second one for both of them. She has a child of seven by her first marriage. Alice is very quiet and seems rather self-contained. Arthur, on the other hand, talks a lot and seems to think of himself as a typical salesman who has no fear of others. From his point of view Arthur describes the problem as Alice's lack of time for him. He feels he is far down on her list of priorities. He is becoming increasingy successful in his business but feels that Alice won't listen to his "dragon-slaying" stories. The problem from Alice's point of view is what she calls "his ego" and his sensitivity to anything that might be understood as critcism. She fears that she can't be emotionally responsive enough to meet his needs, so she backs even farther away.

There are variations on these central themes in their individual histories and the history of their relationship, but this is enough to see something of the particular pain they feel and the way their relationship seems to accentuate it. Thinking about their situation psychologically, one can see Arthur's emotional hunger driving him to be overaggressive and demanding, exhausting himself emotionally and being left vulnerable and hurt when diappointed by Alice and other people. Alice, in contrast, seems to have enough to get by emotionally, so she plays everything safe, seldom risking herself with Arthur or other persons. She has learned to be careful and to try to hold on to what she has. Alice's and Arthur's personalities both complement and frustrate each other. However, in trying to discuss "the problem," I have emphasized the latter rather than the former.

Theologically, Alice's sin is more likely to be in what she has not done rather than what she has done. Arthur, on the other hand, is more likely to have done what he ought not to have done. In both cases, the sin is more than behavioral. It cannot be dealt with simply by doing a little more of this or a little less of that. All of Alice and all of Arthur are involved. In order to deal with either the sin or the psychological need and the relational problem both an approach to the specifics of the problem and the general estrangement or "no health" are needed.

It is important to make clear at this point that my designating Alice and Arthur as sinners is not blaming them for what they have done or not done. It is simply the way things are—at least as informed by my theological under-standing of the human condition. Moreover, from my point of view, there is more potential for dignity and respect for Alice and Arthur in my understanding of them as sinners than in my omitting this dimension and responding only to the psycholog-ical understanding of their problem. If persons are sinners, they are in some kind of responsible relationship to God and to humankind. This points to the possibility of the best in them as well as realistically looking at the worst. In this particular case psychological and theological understanding do not preclude but amplify each other.

When pastoral counselors use theological symbols, such as sin, in interpreting cases, they raise the question, In what way should such language be used with counselees? Thus far, I have used my understanding of sin to enrich my own perception of Alice and Arthur's situation. I have not talked with them in these terms. The decision to do so will be a clinical judgment based on the circumstances of the counsel-ing process. When I believe that the use of theological symbols will deepen Alice and Arthur's understanding of their life situation, rather than being self-justifying for me, I will use them. Sometimes I use theological terms in the kind of diagnostic feedback summarized at the end of this chapter. In the case of Alice and Arthur, I made the clinical judgment that my use of such terms would be misunderstood at this point and might be better understood later. It would be too easy for Alice and Arthur to see these terms as condemning them and confirming them in their situation rather than freeing them to do something about it. When we develop a more common language with each other, the same terms can be experienced in a different way. I discuss more on this issue in the final chapter of this book.

Likeness and Differentness

Thus far I have presented the common and the unique in terms of its occurrence within the individual, the dialectic between "no health" and the things counselees have done and not done. Another dimension of this issue has to do with the degree to which the specifics of my problem is unique to me or is common with other persons. When counselees come to a helping person of any type they hope, sometimes desperately, that their problem will sound familiar. One of the things I have heard from counselees again and again when I asked them in the second interview to reflect on what happened in our first session together is their relief that I seemed familiar with their problem. On the other hand, I have heard, less frequently, but consistently that I seemed a bit too familiar with the problem. Probably, I have heard this less frequently because many of these people did not come back for a second interview. In some way or other I was not respectful of the uniqueness of their pain. I acted too quickly as if their pain was like everybody else's.

William James' comments in his great work, *The Varieties of Religious Experience,* can help most of us in our response to the human situation:

> The first thing the intellect does with an object is to class it along with something else. But any object that is infinitely important to

us and awakens our devotion feels to us also as if it must be *sui generis* and unique. Probably a crab would be filled with a sense of personal outrage if it could hear us class it without ado or apology as a crustacean, and thus dispose of it. "I am no such thing," it would say; "I am MYSELF, MYSELF alone."[9]

The process of pastoral counseling, begun during the evaluation interview or interviews, is one which moves dialectically between the realities of "I am myself, myself alone," and "I am like everyone else." As one might expect, there is good news and bad news, both grace and judgment on both sides of the dialectic. The question that guides the pastoral counselor in the diagnostic process is, How is this person unique, and how is he or she like others? What many of us learned from Carl Rogers was a resistance to quick classification and a challenge to discover the "internal frame of reference of the client, to perceive the world as the client sees it, to perceive the client himself as he is seen by himself"[10] can assist us in maintaining an appropriate balance between the two poles of the diagnostic question. Unless one has gained some significant access to looking at things the way the counselee does, understanding that person's human situation will be significantly limited to those things which are common to all of us.

One of the couples who came to me for help with their marital relationship did so initially because of the wife's disappointment with her husband's lack of involvement with her and the children. He was an executive with a soft drink company and had had phenomenal success moving up the corporate ladder. The relationship pattern of the wife's feeling competitive with the husband's work was familiar to me, so familiar, perhaps, that I found myself unable to understand the intensity of the wife's feeling.

From my external perspective the husband did not seem to be irresponsible. As I compared him to other "corporate husbands," in fact, he seemed admirable, but he was clearly unappreciated for what he had accomplished at work. Only as I listened carefully to the wife discuss the deeper values in her life did I understand her when she said, "If only he were with a company that produced something worthwhile. It seems such a waste for him to be spending his life selling people soda pop." Until I heard the meaning of those words, I responded to the externals of the situation from the point of view of my own life situation and failed to understand her pain. The issue is not whether or not this woman is "right" in feeling as she does; it is understanding what she does feel and responding to it.

It is also important to be able to see and respond to what is common in a person's human situation as well as what is unique. In a taped lecture on psychotherapy and the human condition, Sheldon Kopp[11] observed, "everybody wants to be special," and he proceeds to show the ineffectiveness and frustration in that claim. Virtually everyone seeking help feels in some way or another, "I am the only one to whom this has happened, and I need special attention." This is not usually said openly, nor is it the only thing the counselee feels. It is present, however, in the counselee's anxiety, however it may be expressed. In the biblical story of Elijah on Mount Horeb, one can observe the same kind of self-righteousness, isolation, and paranoia that we see in our counselees:

> It is enough; now, O Lord, take away my life; for I am not better than my fathers. . . . I have been very jealous for the Lord God of hosts: for the children of Israel have forsaken thy covenant, thrown down thine altars, and slain thy prophets with the sword; and I, even I only, am left; and they seek my life, to take it away. (I Kings 19:4b, 10 KJV)

The claim of specialness in that passage is frighteningly familiar. "All is lost. I am not special after all, but just like everyone else. I have been good, but the bad guys have won and are after me. Why can't someone take better care of me?" I do not claim that this is accurate biblical exegesis. I do claim that it is an accurate clinical picture of the common, human problem of wanting to be special and experiencing the isolation of that specialness.

The pastoral counselor's task is to respect the need to be special and to try to understand the particular expressions of that need when it is encountered. The burden of the pastoral relationship, the diagnostic process, and the process of counseling itself are to help the Elijahs, or whomever, to discover, without losing the sense of their unique value, that in fact there are seven thousand in Israel like them. They are not really the only ones with that diagnostic picture or pain.

I use the term, "burden" in connection with pastoral relationship to indicate the difficulty of this task. One cannot simply tell troubled persons that they are suffering with the human condition like everyone else. The tension between the common and the unique must be maintained throughout the counseling process, so that the seekers may discover in moments of insight and satisfaction that their problems and possibilities are unique, and are also like everyone else's. If the process is short-circuited and the counselee is merely told this, he will, as Walker Percy has suggested, "Receive the news from his high seat of transcendence as one more item of psychology, throw it into his immanent meat-grinder, and wait to see if he feels better."[12] He probably won't.

Diagnosis as a Way of Talking About One's Human Situation

The quotation from Percy does, however, reintroduce the question, How does knowledge about a particular human situation contribute to the changing of it? How does that knowledge help the counselor and the counselee? Diagnosis in pastoral counseling is not the same as classification.[13] It has very little to do in identifying a particular neurotic illness so that a particular procedure appropriate to that illness may be applied. Diagnosis is, rather, a way of thinking and talking about a particular person's, couple's, or family's life situation that will help them break the pattern of thinking, feeling, and acting in unproductive, stereotypical ways. Knowledge contributes to change by making available previously unperceived choices and possibilities which may be felt, thought about, and acted upon.

Diagnostic knowledge is a social construction of reality growing out of the dialogue between counselor and counselee which informs and is informed by the way in which the counselee experiences the world. Roy Schafer[14] sees therapy moving through increasingly responsible and useful constructions of reality, from an essentially passive construction, such as that in the case of the woman "to whom everything had happened that could possibly happen" (see pp. 140-41) to more active constructions in which the counselee is seen as a mover and changer of things.

An initial pastoral counseling interview or interviews is a way of beginning this process. Pastoral counselors attempt to hear and demonstrate their understanding of the way a person has constructed his or her world, give an alternate understanding that is enough like the counselee's way of putting things together that it can be accepted as being accurate, and gently give back to the counselee the ongoing task of reconstructing his or her world and living in it. Successful therapy, according to James Hillman[15] is a "collaboration between fictions"—a revisioning of the counselee's story into a more intelligent, more imaginative plot that, in effect, creates a more interesting and challenging world in which to live. It involves the recovery of one's myths—those stories that tell who one is and why—and an activating of the dialectic between what is common and unique in one's life.

The diagnostic interviews in pastoral counseling are a way of constructing a road map which may be used by both pastor and counselee in traversing the life situation and/or counseling ahead. If counseling is pursued beyond the evaluation, such interviews have value in creating a language to be used in the therapeutic situation. If counseling terminates after such an interview or interviews, the road map constructed may be used by the counselee for the living of life itself without a counseling relationship. In either case, the process of putting together a new construction of one's life situation that is continuous with old constructions but lead beyond them, seems to me to have significant value.

But how is this general, philosophical understanding of diagnosis related to the nomenclature of staff conferences within both community mental health centers and pastoral counseling centers? How much diagnostic data does a pastor need to have at his or her fingertips? The general answer is that the more pastors are involved in the specialized area of mental health and psychotherapy the more they need to know. In order to participate in interdisciplinary conferences or to function effectively in a mental health setting, one must know the language of that setting.

In addition to that, the various descriptions of what makes up a psychological diagnostic category contribute significantly to a more general knowledge of the human situation. The value of religious history in psychiatric diagnosis has been described by Draper,[16] and the use of theological categories for understanding human experiencing has been emphasized by Pruyser in such a way as to underscore the importance of the pastor's own area of knowledge in describing the human situation. My concern here is not to devalue the importance of psychological diagnostic knowledge, but to present an alternative way of thinking about the issue which seems to me more related to the pastoral diagnostic interview and then to a method of bringing this understanding of the human situation into the process of counseling and of life.

In discussing how to begin pastoral counseling with a particular individual or couple, I present a structure for a pastoral diagnostic interview that has been useful to me for a number of years. Although the persons with whom I have used this particular structure have been seen in a pastoral counseling center, I believe that the general pattern of the interview is also useful in a parish context. Most initial counseling interviews conducted by ministers who are not specialists in pastoral counseling have as their major fault a lack of structure, too much ventilation of both fact and feeling, and not enough insight into what has been shared.

Pastors, whatever their training and wherever they work, can do a better job in their ministry if they have a familiar context of understanding in which to interpret what they hear from their counselees. The reader who is familiar with the literature of counseling and psychotherapy will recognize the sources of much of what I will present, and I will attempt to document some of them. In many cases, however, my ideas have been assimilated from many sources, including supervision and consultation, and a direct reference cannot be made.

A Structure for Pastoral, Diagnostic Interview

Making a counselee as comfortable as possible in the room where the counseling is to take place and beginning the interview with some statement about what I already know about his or her situation seem important to me. In the case of a parishioner some of the background material that is known can be omitted, but the immediate circumstances of how the interview was set up and why should be reviewed very briefly.[17]

The importance of this is twofold: (1) it begins the interview with honesty and openness and provides an example of it; and (2) it attempts to convey the idea that "I have not heard any gossip about you which I am concealing. What I will respond to will not be something I have heard from other sources, but what you tell me about yourself." One might think of this procedure as dispelling paranoia or building trust. However others think about it, I have found it to be very valuable in what is often called "establishing the working alliance."[18]

After this initial statement by the pastoral counselor and any resulting dialogue about it, I find it useful to start the main portion of the interview with the question, "What hurts?" I believe that my use of the question comes from Virginia Satir, who begins her book on *Conjoint Family Therapy*[19] with the statement, "Family therapists deal with family pain," and from my own application of the biblical image of Isaiah 53, "The pastoral counselor is acquainted with grief."[20] That direct question is often a little more than a beginning relationship can handle because it moves so quickly to the feeling dimension of the person's life. It can be hedged or softened by something like, "What's going on with you now that is getting to you enough to cause you to ask for help?"

The focus here is still on the present and aimed toward the affective dimension of life, but not quite as demanding. The advantage of the question, however it is framed, is that it begins immediately to tell a person what pastoral counseling is about, namely, sharing one's pain with a caring person and developing a relationship in which the pain and joy of life can be explored. The question also gets to some elements in two of the "magic questions," What are you looking for? and Why now? which can be more effectively discussed in their own terms later in the interview. Introduced here, they often lead to an intellectual discussion that can miss the person's pain.

In the case of Alice and Arthur, presented earlier in the chapter, Arthur's pain was in the pressure he felt to provide security for Alice and her daughter and what he perceived as a lack of appreciation of his efforts. Alice's pain was in her insecurity about Arthur's changing jobs and in her own feeling of inadequacy in meeting Arthur's emotional demands. In the case of a couple, it is important that each have an opportunity to try to talk about his or her feelings, the other listening without much interruption. (Cf. chapter 5.) With an individual or couple, the initial focus is on the *now*, rather than the past, and how things are affecting this person at the moment.

A great deal of time should be given to this initial question and to variations of it that attempt to get at the issue of how this particular person is experiencing life. The answer to this question gives a more useful diagnostic picture than any other. It is a description of the human situation that is to be addressed by the pastoral counseling. The person's capacity to respond to that kind of question also has diagnostic implications. If he or she can respond almost immediately to a question about affect, his or her own feelings, then the person will quickly begin to receive benefit from the counseling process. That person already "knows" how to get something from another human being. If he/she has difficulty doing this, then the pastoral counselor knows that the process will be slower and will involve more teaching on what relationships are about.

The most common avoidance of the question of what hurts will be in the counselee's quick shift of focus to something outside himself or something about himself that he does not see as a part of his "real self." "I am here because my wife is bothered by my temper," was an answer to the question which quickly presented two external causes of the problem and indicated that this would be "a long hour." (My sense of time seems directly related to the amount of feeling expressed in an interview. The less personal and appropriate affect expressed, the longer the hour. I recall one person to whom I asked all the questions I usually ask in two sessions in twenty minutes and then did not know what to do with the remaining time. I referred him to our consulting psychiatrist, and he finished his usual diagnostic interview in fifteen minutes. I did not do well with this counselee.)

A review of my notes on several hundred counselees reveals the response to this first question, or my struggle to get some response to it, took up a great deal of time in the first session. After trying at least twice to get some kind of affective response, I back away from it, encourage the person to tell me the story in his or her own words, and then come back to the "How did that hurt you?" question later. Even if the material presented in lieu of the pain involves more information than feeling, I have found it helpful to try to encourage the counselee to focus on what's going on in the present and, if not, to relate what he is experiencing now, what's happening now? Moving from present to past is more useful than going the other way, because it is more like the optimum process of counseling, in which the counselee feels something now, associates it with something in the past, and connects the two together with implications for the future. This process will be explored in detail in chapter 8.

Another important question which is in the pastoral counselor's mind when he or she enters into a discussion of the counselee's pain is the degree to which this person can tell a story about himself/herself. When someone says to me, "I have trouble with relationships," in one sense I know what he or she means. At least I know what the words mean. In a more important sense, however, I am farther away from the counselee than before the question was answered, because what I heard does not tell me anything about that particular person, and I must try again to experience her. I usually do this by saying something like, "Can you tell me a story about that?" If the person seems put off by the idea of storytelling, I may counter with the request that she illustrate what she means by the generalization. That is a second choice to get at the same thing, because it seems to assume that the story is secondary to the generalization when it is actually the other way around.

Revelation of meaning and growth in relationship occur in stories rather than abstractions. If I am involved in a longer term counseling experience with a person who brings in dreams, I encourage the person to bring in the story of the dream without interpretation or explanation, so that we can experience the story together. My concern in counseling at every stage in the process, however, is to help a person listen to the story his/her life is telling and to become curious about it. The diagnostic interview gives a picture of just how difficult this is going to be, or if it is possible at all.

Following a thorough exploration of "what's going on now" with an emphasis on pain and on stories that illustrate the counselee's way of dealing with the pain, the interview can move away for awhile from the central issue and deal with more external data about the person that can help in the understanding of the pain and personal life-style. If the pain has been primarily in the area of person or family relationships, the pastoral counselor can appropriately back away from that for awhile and find out about the situation at work. What is the person getting out of that area of life? How well is he or she functioning there? Is there some parallel between what's happening at work and what's happening at home?

It seems natural to me to move from an inquiry about job

satisfaction to job stability. Has this person moved around from job to job never quite finding the right thing? Then the stability question can be extended into the area of place. Does the counselee have a place to be "from"? Is any one place more home to him than any other? Did the family of origin move around a lot or stay in one place? What was that place or places like? If there was a lot of moving, it is sometimes useful to get from the counselee a life itinerary, noting how many months or years the person stayed in each place, and to bring that itinerary up to the present.

At this point in the interview I usually try to find out something about the external circumstances of the counselee's family of origin and wait until later to find out what kind of persons the parents were. Sometimes the counselee begins to talk about the parents here more than I want him/her to. In such a case, I usually listen for awhile and then tell the person that I want to move on now and come back to that later. It's not that I think the family of origin is unimportant, but I am concerned early in a counseling relationship for the counselee to describe life in terms of his/her own experiencing, not that of the parents.

On of the useful ways to avoid getting prematurely hung up on the family of origin is to move to the area of health. Whether it is good or bad most people seem relatively comfortable talking about their physical health. It is important for a pastoral counselor, whether in parish or counseling center, to know about a person's attitude toward his body. Are body and spirit at peace with each other and experienced in some unity or is there a feeling that the body must be "treated" in some way to be brought in line? Has there been illness or disease in the present family or family of origin? Has one of the children been seriously ill and, if so, how did each parent handle that crisis? What about alcohol and drugs, prescription or recreational? Is chemical manipulation of the body likely to affect the counseling relationship or life situation in some significant way? Does the counselee expect the pastoral counselor to maintain a medical-type responsibility for what happens in counseling, to have something readily available to deal with the pain if it becomes too intense? Do the person's physical symptoms and type of illness give any clue to the life-style of the person?

The next area to be explored in an initial interview is the counselee's or couple's sexuality. If this has not already come up as part of the pain discussed earlier, it is important to discuss sexuality in a matter-of-fact way in the initial interview in order to lay the groundwork to discuss it in more detail later on. Pastors who are counseling members of their own parish may wish to wait until the counselee brings up the area of sexual living himself/herself, because the pastor's knowledge of the parishioner's sexual behavior may be embarrassing for the parishioner or pastor when they meet in relationships outside the counseling hour.

In general, however, a matter-of-fact discussion of sexuality, introduced by asking a question such as, "How are things in your sexual living?" does more to reduce anxiety than to raise it. The pastor has indicated that it is OK to talk about sex, so if the counselee has significant anxiety about this, he or she does not have to take the responsibility for bringing the matter up. My own practice is to do a "once-over-lightly" approach in a first interview and indicate that we will come back to this later on. Often in my experience a person or couple will indicate in a first interview that their sexual living is going well, but later they will say, "Oh, by the way, what we told you in the first interview wasn't quite right," and will proceed to discuss some significant pain in that area. It is important to lay the groundwork for later discussion.

I find a discussion of religion to come naturally after a discussion of sex, and I use a parallel question to the sexual one, "Where are you in your religious living?" The question assumes that persons have a religious life, just as the previous question assumed that they had a sexual life. My concerns here are some of the same ones expressed by Paul Pruyser in identifying a set of religious diagnostic variables in his book, *The Minister as Diagnostician.*[21] What is sacred to the

159

counselee? How does he or she sense this being a world ordered by God's providence? Does this person believe in some kind of purposeful movement of history, including his or her history? Is there some sense of grace as unexpected discovery of goodness of life? Does the counselee have a sense of responsibility, of being able to sin? These are some of the areas of religious life suggested by Pruyser's provocative little book. I seldom ask more than one or two of these questions directly. Many people have at least as much difficulty discussing their religious life as they do their sexual life; sometimes this is particularly true when they are asked to discuss them with a minister. I find it useful, therefore, to touch on them lightly the first time around, simply indicating their importance, and save detailed exploration until later.

Related, I think, to the question about religion is a more general question of life assessment, which begins to move the first interview toward closure. "As you look at your life—not just now, but your whole life—do you see a stable course of events in relation to which your present pain is an exception, or is it more of a series of ups and downs with many hurts and crises?" The question attempts to put the particular situation in which the person is asking for help in perspective. It also suggests that a part of the counseling process is learning to sit back and take the long view as well as being caught up in the present.

Another overview question that should be brought up at this time, if some understanding of the issue has not come out earlier, is, Who are the people who have helped you along the way? Who has been important in making you who you are? First, persons in the past and then those in the present should be identified. What kind of network of supporting and sustaining relationships has the counselee had? What is the degree of his or her isolation? Persons were created for neighbor-hood; therefore, if the counselee is aware of and sustained by his or her significant relationships, the counseling process, which is itself relational, will proceed much more easily.

Finally, the initial interview moves back to the question

with which it began, this time phrased something like this: "Tell me again what's hurting you most and why you're here. I may be able to hear your pain a little differently now that I know more about you." Very often the counselee's response to this now will be somewhat different from the one given at the beginning. Moreover, the pastoral counselor will have a more adequate framework of understanding in which to perceive both the pain and the hopes expressed about what the counseling can do to relieve it.

The pastoral counselor has structured the interview so that it has moved full circle. What now? I believe that he/she should give a brief summary of what has been heard and then give the counselee/s an opportunity to ask questions about the summary and about anything else that the counselee/s may be curious about: the pastoral counselor, the structure of any future counseling sessions, fees, if any, the possibility of bringing in consultants. The more open the pastor can be about the structure in which the counseling will take place, the easier it will be for both counselor and counselee to work productively within it.

A "Report-Back" of Diagnostic Impressions

But what of the content of the summary of the first interview? Let me be specific about this. The following is a reconstruction of a first session report-back to a couple whom I shall call Jim and Joni:

> I think you have good reason to be here, and I congratulate you on being wise enough to recognize that there were some things that you needed to work on. You've been married long enough (five years) to have experienced some of the ways that you can hurt each other, but you are trying to do something about it now before the patterns are fully set. It will be easier now than it will be later. Jim, you are the one who telephoned me, but it seems to have been at Joni's insistence, so I'll talk about her first. She seems to me to be feeling her pain more intensely than you. Yours seems to be tucked away deeper inside.

Joni, you have described yourself as a very meticulous person, bothered by everything from Jim's messy hair to a messy desk at the office. You're fearful that the way Jim is will reflect badly on you. But you've been tight and tense a long time. The ulcer you mentioned was there before you met Jim. Some of the unresolved tension seems to me to be related to your leaving the Catholic Church. There are some things still to be dealt with. It's hard for you to feel OK with the world, to trust things. Some of the tension carries over to your sexual life. Intercourse sounds like it's often more work than play. Maybe a good way to focus the issue for you is to say that you have difficulty in trusting: Jim, the world, yourself. I think of counseling for you as a way of developing your trust in relationships.

Jim, as I've said, you seem to keep things tucked down deeper. Your feelings aren't as available as Joni's. If we go on with this, I'll be looking for them. Right now you seem to be letting her feel things for you. You describe your pain as being bothered by Joni's. I don't doubt that you are, but I am trying to get at the way you experience things. You are more disorganized than Joni, and you probably married her partly because you needed some of what she's got. You found her at a chaotic period in your life, and her way of being seems to have stabilized you. If that stays the primary way that you relate, however, you're gong to end up being married to a mother rather than a wife and that may make your sexual experience more dificult. You're better at trusting than Joni is. The issue for you is more in getting in touch with the person you are and trust and being willing and able to express that. This includes being more available to Joni without having to feel trapped. That's the way I see it at this point. These are just impressions based on what you've told me. I suppose it's a kind of a caricature, accentuating the major features I see. Does it sound like you to you, and do you have any questions?

That was a fairly long speech. More often than not this kind of summary or report-back is interrupted along the way and is more dialogical. Sometimes I structure it in that way, so that there will not be so many of my words to listen to at one time. The intent of the summary is to indicate that I have been listening and to reveal some of the ways I listen and some of the language I use to think about people's pain. At this point in a counseling relationship, the most everyday language available seems the best, language that is neither too psychological or theological. The reader noted that I began by commending Jim and Joni on their asking for help, suggesting that what they may perceive as weakness, I perceive as strength, a strength that they can call on in dealing with the issues that give them pain. I attempt to talk openly about pain, demonstrating my belief that that's the way life is, that pain is something to grow from, not simply to escape from. With a couple, I attempt to say something about each one as well as about the relationship. As I presented in detail in the previous chapter, the pastoral counselor's task is to deal with all three.

Readers who are specialists in pastoral counseling and parish ministers as well have no doubt by this time raised serious questions about the procedure I have described. For some it may not be detailed enough, for others it may be much more than they want to get into. My purpose in being this specific has not been to suggest my way of doing things as normative, but to stimulate questions as to what is most useful for a particular pastoral counselor in defining the situation to which pastoral counseling is addressed.

Some kind of diagnosis or definition of the situation will be taking place in any first interview. My concern is that this be as usable as possible to the pastor. I have serious questions about whether "just listening" to the problem is adequate for any pastoral counselor, however much involvement he or she may have in this field of ministry. Listening proceeds more satisfactorily if an adequate context for listening is developed as a part of the listening. This means an active, even aggressive listening, which is dialogical in nature. There is, optimally, a mutual sharing of ways to describe the human situation. It helps avoid what still seems to me to be the most common problem of the beginning pastoral counselor, listening rather passively while a counselee dumps a problem on him/her and then feeling the demand to come up with an "answer" to it. The procedure I have described attempts to have both parties in the encounter involved in the definition of the situation and the response to it.[22]

Referral

The most obvious omission from the discussion as it has proceeded thus far is an explicit consideration of referral. And, judging by the kind of questions I hear in ministers' conferences on pastoral counseling, the issue does need to be addressed. The major reasons a pastoral counselor may decide to refer counselees to another professional person are: (1) lack of time; (2) training which is insufficient or inappropriate for the situation at hand; and (3) too much involvement with the counselee or his or her family to allow the pastoral counselor to function professionally as well as personally. Each of these reasons may prevent pastors from offering themselves freely in the relationship. All of them may apply to both parish ministers and to those who practice their ministry in a pastoral counseling center.

Pastors may deal with the issue of lack of time either in the first telephone call or may wait until the first interview and then interpret the limits of their present situation. I prefer to see persons whom I know fairly well once and then make a referral. Under those circumstances, I can know enough about the troubling circumstances to make a more adequate referral. With respect to the issue of training, which is insufficient or inappropriate to the situation, the pastoral counselor, however experienced or specialized he or she may be, needs to acknowledge this openly and use those circumstances to make it easier for the person to see someone else.

The old idea that a particular person may be "too sick" for a pastor to help seems to me to be no longer useful—at least in that form. If pastors use the "magic questions" in structuring and diagnosis, then they are free to discuss openly what the counselee appears to be looking for and how that fits with what they see going on. Most important, the "magic questions" should help pastors realize that just because persons come to them for help does not mean that they have to take responsibility for the lives of these people. Rather, the pastor's task is to offer a caring relationship in which the counselee can be assisted in finding what he or she is looking for whether it is personal affirmation or psychiatric hospitalization. Referral takes place as a part of that process of identifying what one is looking for and what resources for help are available.

With respect to the issue of too much involvement with the person, there seems to be two aspects of this. The first has to do with relationships to this person or those close to the person outside the counseling relationship. A discussion of this in relation to the concept of transference appears in the next chapter, but there may be reasons apparently unrelated to transference which would cause the pastoral counselor to refer. Sometimes I am immediately aware of these and can tell the potential counselee over the telephone that this is the case. At other times, I am not aware of them until I sit down with the person and discuss his or her situation. Recently a young man, whose father, now deceased, had been associated with our counseling center, requested pastoral counseling with me. Although I doubted my prior relationship to his father, whom I had known well, would allow me to work with him, it seemed important that we spend an hour discussing both his and my situation. We did so—I think to the advantage of both of us—and I referred him to another pastoral counselor on our staff.

In other circumstances the overinvolvement with the counselee may be only potential, but it is important that the pastoral counselor attempt to see this from the outset. If, for example, the counselee is struggling with an issue in his or her life which is too much related to something that I am struggling with, it is important that I make an appropriate referral to another counselor. I recall a time when two of my children were in the process of breaking away from home, and I found that in dealing with young people of the same age, struggling with similar issues from their side of the relationship, I could not effectively untangle my feelings from theirs. My feelings did not have to be suppressed—they helped me in other situations—but they did limit me for a period of time in the type of situation in which I could use my feelings effectively. Through supervision or consultation, the pastoral counselor can learn, in most cases, to recognize potential overinvolvement and avoid it through effective referral.

Finally, if referral does take place, it is more effective if it can be to a person rather than an agency or clinic. Encouraging someone to go to a person whom the pastor knows and believes to be effective can extend the pastoral relationship rather than abort it. That person may be practicing in an agency or clinic, but the referral should be made to a particular person there. This obviously means that in order to refer effectively a pastor needs to be acquainted with particular professional persons, rather than just knowing about agencies. In that way one relationship can build upon another.

Summary

I have attempted to address the issue of diagnosis or definition of the situation to which pastoral counseling is a response. My concern has been to do this primarily in terms of the pastoral, rather than the psychological or psychiatric, tradition. Obviously, this attempt has been more of a matter of emphasis than a sharp definition of what is pastoral and what is psychiatric. My discussion has involved both the theological and the psychological understanding of what it means to be human and the broad philosophical question of how knowledge is related to change. Part of our trouble, as Walker Percy suggests, is wanting to know what our trouble is. I believe that the type of knowledge of "trouble" (diagnosis) I have discussed can indeed lead to change: through the development of relationship; through *owning* one's own story; and by discovering what can and cannot be changed in one's human situation. Now I move on to the most important ingredient in pastoral counseling—the relationship.

Chapter Seven

What Heals?—Relationship in Pastoral Counseling

If any healing occurs through pastoral counseling it occurs through relationship. Much of what I have said previously can be seen as growing out of that conviction. Because pastors must respond to people where they are in the midst of specific human problems, pastoral care and counseling are too easily identified with problem-solving. Although some knowledge of problems is necessary to communicate with persons in need, the pastor's vocation is not to "cure" these many and varied problems. His or her responsibility is to affirm through relationship that none of the human hurts listed in Romans 8 or those on our own list can separate us from the love of God as revealed in Christ.

The offering of relationship, however, is not a simple matter. Much of the literature of psychotherapy is a testimony to that fact. My purpose in this chapter is to examine some of the things that have been learned about the importance of relationship in psychotherapy within the context of the pastoral relationship. To begin this examination, it may be useful to look again at the case that was presented in chapter 1.

Dimensions of the Pastoral Relationship

Joanne described me as "father, lover, and religious person." Some of the important meaning of being a "religious person," someone representative of the many meanings of the Christian tradition, was discussed in chapter 2 in terms of the necessity of the pastoral counselor's visibility. The emphasis in this chapter is on the other two terms: father and lover. To function competently as a pastoral counselor, whatever the context for ministry, the pastor must be able to be both.

Historically, the priest has been father, but the male symbol is not of primary importance. The pastoral counselor at his or her symbolic and representational best may be a parent of either sex. I remember my chagrin some years ago when I discovered that the attractive young woman with whom I was counseling was relating to me as if I were her grandmother. Grandmother was the only one who had expected anything from her morally or ethically, and my value to her as a pastoral counselor depended on my willingness to work with what was there for her, rather than to insist on being myself.

Joanne also referred to me as a "lover." I understand this quite literally as meaning, "one who has the capacity to love." What she is saying is that my feelings are available to her, and that I have found a way to love her and to let her love me without my having to become directly involved in her day-to-day life. Pastoral counselors must be personally available to give and to grow through the awareness of and use of their own feelings. There are times when detachment is important and necessary, but pastoral counseling should involve depth of relationship and personal involvement. In the case with Joanne, she moved through her pain to respond to mine. In doing so, she rediscovered her "courage to be" and was able to look up at the dark clouds and black umbrellas with a new will to live in the face of her dying and mine.

I move now to explore in some detail how "religious persons" (pastors) express themselves in relationships as "fathers" and "lovers." My method of doing this is, first, to identify the *parent* dimension of the pastoral relationship with the psychoanalytic tradition in psychotherapeutic literature and to suggest some of the important implications of that tradition for the pastoral relationship. Second, I identify the "lover" dimension of the relationship with the experiential tradition in psychotherapeutic literature and suggest some of the implications of that tradition. Both of these traditions have contributed to my formation as a pastoral counselor, and I have repeatedly seen evidence of their contribution to my colleagues.

The difference of my own position from many other pastoral counseling specialists is that I do not believe that we have to choose between these two traditions. Rather, it is my contention that each contributes to the understanding of an important dimension of the pastoral relationship that should not be left out of the process of ministry. The relationship between the two dimensions may sometimes be dialectic, i.e., one yielding to the other as the need arises at any time in the counseling process. The relationship between the two dimensions may also be sequential, i.e., beginning with the more parental dimension of the relationship and later becoming more expressive, reciprocal, and existential. Although I do not claim to be clear about the relationship between the two, I am sure that in the light of my own experience as a pastoral counselor, I am not willing to give up either dimension. I am further convinced that these traditions contribute as much to the meaning of "pastoral" as to "counselor."

The Parent Dimension

I begin with the parent[1] dimension, because the discipline of learning or developing this dimension of relationship in oneself offers a more adequate structure for understanding the pastoral counseling process than the lover dimension. The former is more historical; the latter more existential. In one sense, at least, the "parent" provides a structure within which the "lover" can express itself. I explore the parent dimension through the use of five psychoanalytic concepts: the primary concept of transference and the related concepts of establishing the working alliance, abstinence, resistance, and counter-transference. In order to make clear to the reader that I am importing concepts from another context because of their practical value in interpreting pastoral work instead of their theoretical importance in psychotherapy, I begin this discussion with an incident from the general practice of ministry, not specialization in pastoral counseling.

The following material was tape-recorded a number of years ago when I was studying lay visitation in a small church. This particular evening much of the discussion focused on the church's pastor, most of what was said came from a layman whom I will call Elwood:

> One of the things I don't like about myself—I can't go to church and enjoy things as they are. I can't even— I find some fault in Jim (the minister) or if he's preaching a good sermon I'll worry my blame head off because the people aren't enjoying it. I can't take things as they are. Jim says, uh, he can stand up to all of it; not me. I mean, the way that—if he's preaching a lousy sermon, I'm worried about him. And if people are not listening I'm worried about them. And I'm in between worrying about both of them and can't do a confounded thing about it but listen. . . .
>
> He'll come up next week and preach about our uncles being monkeys or something and he . . . One week I'm with him—he's on the Old Testament—plain old gospel like it's easy for a man like me to understand, and next week he don't know whether he believes in evolution or he don't believe in it. . . . And I don't like to talk Bible with you because you've got a theology on the Bible that you can work anyway. . . .
>
> Well, a preacher—I was brought up—a preacher, what he believes, he better believe it and make me believe it. But he ain't ever certain about nothing. He can get a beehive stirred up and the—and then step back. . . . A preacher should give you a school of thought and you take a school of thought and go away with it because he's your preacher. And then if you don't agree with him, he's not your preacher. He has humility but he won't display it. He'll, uh, sit back and say, "Well, uh, I've overdone it last quarter, and this quarter I'll sit back and let the lid blow off. Just let them stick their feet in their mouth." If he'd show a little humility. I'd stand up at the board meeting and really defend him, but how can I defend him and love him when I think he's two jumps ahead of me all the time, and the congregation. He, he knows our alternatives so why, what little— What can I do to defend him?

You can't protect him so you'll just say, "By grannies, I hope they'll tear him up and maybe he'll get scratched up enough that I can help him sooner or later!" That's the way some people feel about him. He'll keep on, he'll get down in a mess, and then we can help him. But, he, he gets in a mess, and he either gets off to himself or you can't find him or. . . .

Jim will never do any good at that church unless he bows down and, the people won't hurt him—but he's got to be willing for them to hurt him. Then bring him down to the house and feed him on Sunday, and, give him some white shoes and a coat. If he'll get a little humble he'll be loved.[2]

What is going on here? Obviously a great deal. As I reflect on the incident, my first response is that as a group leader today, I would not allow this much feeling to be vented by anyone in a parish setting for fear of later repercussions. In terms of what actually was said, although some of the expectations of the pastor may be unique to this particular person and to small churches in the southeast, I believe that they point to the kind of reactions that exist toward pastors everywhere.

In one of the standard volumes on psychoanalytic technique, Ralph R. Greenson identifies the main characteristic of transference as:

the experience of feelings to a person which do not befit that person and which actually apply to another. Essentially, a person in the present is reacted to as though he were a person in the past. Transference . . . is an anachronism, an error in time. A displacement has taken place; impulses, feelings and defenses pertaining to a person in the past have been shifted onto a person in the present. It is primarily an unconscious phenomenon.[3]

Elwood's reaction to his pastor is not just transference. Except, perhaps, in formal psychoanalytic treatment itself, no response of one person to another is purely that. There are, however, in the minister's role and function, important elements that elicit transference reactions. The pastor necessarily represents authority figures from the parishioner's past, usually those who challenged one way of life and described the importance of another.

A woman counselee whose way of life proclaimed her "liberation" from a rather religious family of origin had indicated to me in the process of my getting to know her that she had no interest in religion and that she had come to me simply because a friend told her I was a good psychotherapist. Early in our relationship however, she dreamed that she was a new teacher in a school that looked like one she had attended as a teen-ager. The principal was conducting a group session to get acquainted with the new teachers, and they were doing "those Mickey-Mouse things you do in education courses." To her surprise when her turn came to tell about herself, the principal asked her to recite her favorite Bible verses. Feeling defensive, she replied that she was not a religious person, but her mother was. When she concluded describing the dream and indicated that she had no immediate associations about it, I commented that she was having a little trouble with my being a minister. After that we had some very useful opportunities to explore some of the things I represented to her.

What is most evident in Elwood's comments is the strength of the pastoral/relationship and its personal quality. Elwood was so involved with the pastor that he couldn't "enjoy things as they are." He worried about the pastor's impact on the congregation but felt helpless to do anything about it. We can only speculate about the reasons for this without having as much information as I had about my counselee with the dream. The important thing is for pastors to be aware of the powerful impact they may have on people. They cannot avoid seeming to be more than they really are.

Moreover, the pastoral relationship is seldom definite and clear-cut as to who does what and when. Pastors work in an interpersonal environment where their function cannot be completely or even satisfactorily delineated by themselves or their parishioners. This produces a tension that both pastor and parishioner attempt to resolve. The layman in this incident first dealt with the ambiguity of his relationship with the pastor by attempting to reduce it to technical procedures that the pastor had either done or not done. He doesn't preach the "plain old gospel like it's easy for a man like me to understand." Or the pastor may be judged technically inadequate because "he ain't ever certain about nothing." The way "I was brought up—a preacher, what he believes, he better believe it and make me believe it. . . . If you don't agree with him, he's not your preacher."

The layman's second way of dealing with the indefiniteness or ambiguity of the pastoral relationship was to reduce it to a friendship in which the pastor's authority could be denied. The pastor's problem in relationships was seen to be a lack of humility. "How can I defend him and love him when I think he's two jumps ahead of me all the time. . . . You can't protect him so you'll just say, "By grannies, I hope they'll tear him up and maybe he'll get scratched up enough that I can help him.' " His anger toward the pastor's authority, probably growing out of his own feelings of inadequacy, builds, and he elaborates the lack of humility theme by proclaiming that the pastor is really not like Jesus.

Much of this can be seen, as Greenson has informed us, as "an anachronism, an error in time" or "a displacement." However we describe it, the pastor must be aware that transference phenomena are out there. He or she cannot be a pastor and deny a pastor's importance to people, however liberated from parental morality or secularized they may seem to be. Being "one having authority" is part of the territory of ministry and its transference dimensions need to be recognized and dealt with rather than denied because they are uncomfortable.

How does a parish minister manage a transference reaction in a parishioner with whom he or she may have regular and sometimes official relationships that affect both the pastor and the church? Certainly, he or she should be aware that the symbolic role of the pastor and its association with early family life and parental figure make such reactions virtually impossible to escape. Pastors cannot really avoid being more than they really are. That being the case, they should recognize that the kind of structured and controlled relationship that is possible in psychotherapy is impossible with parishioners. Confrontations with persons in the parish who, for one reason or another, have developed transference reactions should, when at all possible, take place in groups where there are others who will be reacting to the same situation in a more realistic way.

In contrast to the structured therapeutic situation where the distortion of the relationship may be used to work through unsatisfactory past relationships, in the less structured relationship with a parishioner, the pastor should attempt to be as real, matter-of-fact, and practical as possible. His or her primary concern should be to help the parishioner achieve effective function and reduction in anxiety rather than insight and understanding. The task at hand, rather than the ambiguities of the relationship, should be emphasized.[4] Later in the chapter I explore some of the issues in managing the transference in pastoral counseling with non-parishioners. My concern here has been to point out the presence of transference distortions in the broader pastoral relationship.

Applied to the more narrow pastoral counseling relationship, the parent dimension represented by the psychoanalytic tradition has even more important contributions to make. After listening to hundreds of audiotapes of students and candidates for membership in the American Association of Pastoral Counselors, the question that most frequently came to my mind is this, Is the counselor there or has he or she somehow managed to leave the room? What the listener hears on the tapes of inexperienced pastoral counselors is the counselee's "problem" described at great, sometimes boring, length with no accompanying sense of the counselor's presence. The counselee is talking, but without any apparent awareness that he or she is talking to a particular person. On the tapes in question the pastoral counselor has apparently not been able to teach his counselee how to talk to him/her. What seems to be going on is just talking.

The Working Alliance

The conditions that make it possible for the counselor to be present were discussed in some detail in the chapters on structuring and defining the situation. The task for the pastoral counselors as they move beyond the period of structuring and evaluation is to shift responsibility for the content of the interview to the counselee without losing the relationship established during the evaluation period.

What is referred to in textbooks on psychotherapy as "establishing the working alliance" is begun in the pre-interview structuring, is continued as the counselor becomes familiar with the human situation of the counselee, and is firmly tested during the first sessions after the counselee has decided to go on with the counseling.

Greenson describes the patient's contribution to the establishment of a working alliance as "the capacity to maintain contact with the reality of the analytic situation" and the "willingness to regress into his fantasy world. It is the oscillation between these two positions that is essential for the analytic work."[5] My counselees and those of most pastors would not fulfill these conditions. On the other hand, the couple whose situation I discussed in chapter 1, whom I "could not help," *were* helped to come to terms with the reality of the counseling situation, of what it could and could not offer. They were able to surrender the fantasy of being fully cared for and to accept one of more limited care and concern.

The broader meaning of "willingness to regress into the fantasy world" for most pastoral counseling is most often, in my experience, the counselee's developing curiosity about his or her life rather than "having a problem" to solve. It is broadening the frame of interpreting one's life from the very narrow focus on something "wrong" to an examination of various features of one's life in relation to one another. One does not have to be an appropriate candidate for psychoanalysis in order to do this.

Glenda, for example, was referred to me by her physician

when he could find no medical reason for the various aches and pains she described to him. When she got to the pastoral counseling center she had decided that her problem was her seventeen-year-old son who was smoking pot and that I might help her by telling her what to do. I attempted to focus on her rather than on the son and discovered that at age thirty-five she still felt compelled to see or call her mother every day. She was very fearful of angering her mother and others and had oriented her life around trying to please. Without going into my reasons for making this judgment, I determined that Glenda was not a candidate for either long-term psychotherapy or even weekly counseling interviews. I gave her a "prescription" of things to do before she came back in two weeks. They included such things as: "Talk with your mother no more than three times a week" and "Do something that helps no one but yourself."

When Glenda came back, to my surprise, she had done most of the things on the "prescription." More important, my interest in her life and her problem had helped her get curious about herself, and as a result she brought in some things she wanted to explore. Although it could not be accurately said that she had decided to "regress into her fantasy world," she did seem to be using the counseling relationship to gain courage to explore and expand her life. Interestingly, the thing she had decided to do for herself was to take swimming lessons. One does not have to interpret that action symbolically to see why people like Glenda are a major reason that I am not willing to limit my ministry to the practice of long-term psychotherapy.

I do not recommend this particular technique to other pastoral counselors, but with a person like Glenda it was one way of offering myself in relationship when a more traditional psychotherapeutic stance would not have been understood or received. It does, however, bring us specifically to the question of what the pastoral counselor contributes to the development of a working alliance. Writing from within a psychoanalytic framework, Greenson states:

The most important contribution that the psychoanalyst makes to a good working relationship comes from his daily work with the patient. The analyst's consistent and unwavering pursuit of insight in dealing with any and all of the patient's material and behavior is the crucial factor. Regular and orderly work routines help the patient adjust to some of the strangeness of the psychoanalytic procedures and processes.[6]

Expanding Greenson's understanding to the situation of the pastoral counselor, one can infer that the working alliance is established by introducing the counselee in a systematic way to the ritual and procedures of the counseling situation. It gradually becomes clear to the counselee that he is not a special case, but is going through the same thing that other counselees go through. Pastoral counselors present themselves not as rigid and unbending, but as persons who know what they are doing and have done it before. This is one of the characteristics that interpersonal psychiatrist Harry Stack Sullivan described in discussing the "expert in interpersonal relations"—the ability to give security. Sullivan's contribution to most of us was his ability to treat even his most disturbed patients in a matter-of-fact way which did not allow their anxiety to disrupt his ordered way of going about things. Whether they are doing long-term psychotherapy or a one-time intervention in a crisis, most pastors need to develop a more routine way of offering their pastoral counseling—a way that not only conveys that they care, but also that they have a well thought-out way of responding to human need.

Abstinence

Another concept from psychoanalytic psychotherapy which is useful in developing a broadened understanding of the pastoral relationship is the concept of abstinence. It is infrequently used in the literature of pastoral care. In fact, most of us tend to think of the term as applying primarily to the abstinence from alcoholic beverages. It has important application, however, to understanding the working alliance.

In the context of a therapeutic relationship, abstinence means "not gratifying the patient's infantile and neurotic wishes."[7] Or to put it in Freud's own terms, "Analytic treatment should be carried through, as far as it is possible, under privation—in a state of abstinence."[8] The analyst attempts to maintain the working alliance, facilitate regression and the full development of the transference neurosis, by denying the patient gratifications other than a responsiveness to his or her analytic work. "The therapeutic task," says Tarachow, "can be imposed only by means of a disappointment and by transformation of a real into an *as if* relationship. We force thinking in place of reality: the uninterpreted relationship is reality."[9] "Cruel though it may sound, we must see to it that the patient's suffering . . . does not come to an end prematurely."[10]

Some of these quotations sound quite distant from the concept of care as pastors usually think about it. They are not too distant, however, from the concept of abstinence in the Christian tradition when that concept is broadened beyond not doing something to an understanding of the place of discipline in the Christian life, or, for that matter, in the development of a mature human being. Denial of immediate gratification is an important principle in the development of almost anything. In every situation of pastoral care and counseling, the pastor is faced with the issue of whether to try to give direct satisfaction to the expressed need of the parishioner/counselee or to provide the conditions under which that person can struggle toward the satisfaction of his or her own need.

In a situation of pain or grief, for example, when the parishioner asks in some way, "Why did this happen to me?" the pastor has to make a decision about whether to satisfy the expressed need by giving an "answer" or attempting to be present in that person's struggle to find an answer for himself/herself. In the latter case, the pastor may be thought of as following the rule of abstinence, refusing to satisfy either the other person or himself/herself with an answer.

There are other reasons why one should, in this particular

situation, resist the attempt to give an answer, e.g., the difficulty of hearing an answer during a period of shock or intense anxiety. It can be useful, however, for pastors in a variety of pastoral care situations to think in terms of what the psychoanalyst might call gratification or deprivation—following the rule of abstinence. The way the pastor is guided by that rule will differ from that of the analyst, but there are more parallels than one might first imagine.

> One cannot work analytically unless one can oscillate between the relatively detached analytic position and the more involved physicianly one. The analyst must be a person who can empathize and feel compassion sincerely and yet use restraint. It is necessary at times to inflict pain, to allow the patient to endure suffering. Yet psychoanalytic treatment cannot be accomplished in an atmosphere of unabated grimness, icy detachment, or prolonged cheeriness.[11]

The same issue that Greenson addresses is found in the comments of the layman quoted earlier in the chapter:

> Jim [the pastor] will never do any good at that church unless he bows down and, the people won't hurt him—but he's got to be willing for them to hurt him. Then bring him down to the house and feed him on Sunday, and, and give him some white shoes and a coat. If he'll get a little humble he'll be loved.

There is a fundamental human need to be close to, control, and reduce the threat of anyone in an authority position. The role and function of both physician and pastor make them particularly good targets for this kind of attack. Some of this will be discussed from a somewhat different perspective under the topic of resistance. The point here is that the pastor's own resistance to being brought "down to the house" or adequate discipline on his or her own needs to satisfy and "be loved" can contribute significantly to the development of a working relationship that can extend through long-term pastoral counseling or a long-term pastorate. Much of the pastor's ability to follow the rule of abstinence in order to develop significant relationships may depend on what the standards of the American Association of Pastoral Counselors describe as "having undergone sufficient theological and psychotherapeutic investigation of one's own intrapsychic and interpersonal processes so that one is able to protect the counselee from the pastoral counselor's problems and to deploy oneself to the maximum benefit of the counselee."[12] Learning to move between the relatively detached and a more involved position of relationship is a major task of ongoing supervision and consultation, and it can be informed by the rule of abstinence.

Resistance

The concept of resistance and its relevance for pastoral work, not primarily pastoral counseling, has been explored extensively by James Dittes in *The Church in the Way*.[13] My concern here is to discuss its relevance for the pastoral relationship in pastoral counseling. Because the concept of resistance in psychoanalytic literature relates to virtually every other clinical concept, it is common to find in books on psychoanalytic technique either a large section on resistance or none at all, because the concept is discussed in terms of others. However sophisticated a person may become in the knowledge that resistance is an inevitable part of every change process, he or she finds it difficult to get beyond the feeling, "If only this didn't have to occur. Why can't this one be easy?"

Thus it is not difficult to understand why problem-solving approaches to the human situation are as popular as they are. They allow the helping person to escape before the resistance really sets in. The primitive feeling which is stirred by resistance in any context is that of a song of the forties titled, "Why Don't You Do Right?" or "Here we go again." Pastoral caring and counseling are hard work.

> Every step of the treatment is accompanied by resistance; every single thought, every mental act of the patient's must pay toll to the resistance, and represents a compromise between the forces urging towards the cure and those gathered to oppose.[14]

"It is not the analyst who is being resisted," comments Menninger, "it is the process within the patient which the analyst is encouraging." Menninger continues by identifying "five classical types of resistance."[15] I believe that all of them can be seen in routine pastoral care and counseling, not just in psychoanalytically oriented psychotherapy. I will be discussing the same five types as Menninger, but using primarily my own terminology.

Persons resist change in pastoral counseling because they are fearful of some of the new things that they see and experience in that relationship. What comes to mind in the context of a caring relationship is sometimes too embarrassing to recall, so the counselee manages not to find anything to talk about long after a working alliance has been established. In this type of resistance the counselor fears losing control and experiencing all its painful childhood associations of foolishness and inadequacy.

Another form of resistance is the kind we saw in the layman's feeling about his minister—transference resistance or, *revenge* resistance, as Menninger puts it. Usually, the pastor experiences it as the counselee's response to the pastor's not giving easy answers or not coming through with the expected words or behavior. It is the kind of power struggle in which the counselee says, in effect, "You're not giving me anything, so I won't give you anything." Much of this rebellion is unconscious, but it can be explored by inquiring about the counselee's disappointment in the counseling process and in the counselor. More about this in our discussion on responding to the transference.

The third type of resistance has to do with maintaining the advantages of illness, the joys of getting all this attention. If one gets well or even gets better, he or she is in danger of losing this care. The fourth type of resistance is similar to the third, but is deeper. It is not simply trying to maintain the satisfactions of the immediate caring relationship, but is vigorously holding on to the *status quo* derived from past life patterns. It is, as Freud put it, "beyond the pleasure principle." That explanation is too simple. The powerful conservative principle of the "repetition compulsion" is needed to interpret this type of resistance and a period of "working through" required long after insight is achieved and a decision to change has been made.

The final classic type of resistance is that which seems to grow out of a need for punishment. Persons who have chosen to be their own judge exhibit this type of resistance, seeming to find pleasure in life by passing sentence on themselves. The counselee who threw a pillow at me and angrily screamed, "You're too god-damned understanding!" was expressing this type of resistance along with expressions of transference.

The point of listing forms of resistance—and I have been far from exhaustive in doing this—is to emphasize the patient, painstaking persistence required of those who offer a pastoral counseling relationship to persons in need. Our counselees are too good at thwarting themselves and those who try to help them for any of us to be too comfortable in this type of work. The freedom of not *having* to help, which may be achieved through consultation, is generally one useful way of disarming the resistance. (See chapter 3.) It is very easy for the pastoral counselor unconsciously to fuel the resistance of his/her counselees by needing to give more help than the counselee wants. The first of the "magic questions" is sometimes a valuable tool in beginning to deal with a counselee's resistance. (See chapters 4 and 6.) "During your silence, I found myself thinking back to what you said you wanted from counseling." Or, "It appears that your success in punishing yourself consistently gets in the way of what you say you want to accomplish."

My purpose here is not to detail specific ways of dealing with resistance. This can only come effectively through the supervision of one's actual practice of pastoral counseling. Moreover, the literature on resistance in books dealing with psychotherapy is quite extensive.[16] My intent has not been to duplicate what has already been dealt with more adequately in other places, but to insist that the pastoral counselor must take resistance seriously, much the same way that he or she takes sin seriously.

Resistance and sin are not the same thing, though at times we might like to believe they are. It is comfortable to polarize things and to identify as sinful anything that opposes us or our point of view. Resistance demonstrates the power of the unconscious and, therefore, the complications and convolutions of our sin, but it is not appropriately identified with sin. Resistance is a valuable conservative feature that is used to prevent the loss of important parts of the personality and change for change's sake. For example, it may slow down or prevent the sin of one personality running over and devaluing another in an uncritical effort to *help*.

One of the values of resistance for the pastoral counseling specialist and for the parish pastor in the more varied relationships of ministry is that it crushes the pretensions of those of us who are convinced that we know what is good for people. When resistance appears, it must be analyzed or explored in some way. It has become the agenda and everything else has to wait. It reminds us of the interconnectedness of all events and the kind of flexibility that is necessary when we find something unexpectedly connected to something else. We may want to deal with a religious or sexual problem but find that under the surface somewhere it is connected to a long forgotten embarrassment about spilled milk or some other mess. The fact of resistance is a constant reminder that pastoral care involves the response to whatever is there rather than what we want to be there.

Managing the Transference

The most important type of resistance with which the pastoral counselor must deal is transference resistance. We discussed this previously with respect to its manifestation in a parish situation in terms of a layman's feelings about his minister and as one of the five classic types of resistance, using Menninger's term, "revenge resistance." Transference, however, is much more than resistance. It is resistance in that it manifests itself in the counseling situation—and in a variety of other situations—as a "break in the action." The process stops, and the counselee seems to be somewhere else. He or she is indeed resisting the orderly conduct of the counseling process. In fact, however, the counselee is saying, "What is going on in the counseling right now is not nearly as important as you are to me." If the transference is negative, the same content is being expressed, but it is an attempt to get at the pastoral counselor because he or she disappointed the counselee in some way.

However it is expressed, the transference is saying—among other things, what I have been attempting to say in this chapter, namely, that it is the relationship that heals. In calling attention to the relationship, the counselee is unconsciously reminding his or her counselor of this. And, except perhaps for the most experienced practitioner, most of us need this reminder. It causes less anxiety for the pastoral counselor to go on listening about things "out there" than to face up to the intense feelings that transference brings "in here."

Assuming that the counseling is taking place with a person with whom the pastor has no other significant relationships, transference can be worked out as effectively in a parish as in a counseling center—but not with a parishioner. As we have noted in the incident with the layman, enough transference can go on in ordinary parish life without intensifying it by counseling. With a person with whom the pastor has only the counseling relationship, the pastor can be free to experience with the counselee and interpret the important issues in his or her life.

The specific way the transference is managed will depend on the pastor's training, personal experience as a counselee or patient, and his or her availability to the counselee. Because transference is an intense interpersonal and intrapsychic experience with many potential distortions of reality, the pastoral counselor needs extensive experience in examining his or her *own* ways of distorting things, and, sometimes, to have a consultant who can look at the situation with more detachment, in order to see what is really going on.

What I say here about the actual management of the transference in pastoral counseling will be quite limited. The theoretical literature on the subject is immense and must be examined directly by the serious student of the psychotherapeutic dimensions of pastoral counseling.[17] Learning to manage the transference, however, should be done in a supervisory relationship in which students can look and/or hear themselves on tape and relate the theory to their own style of relationship. Within the context of that relationship, however, certain things about transference come up again and again.

The first of these is the student's difficulty in seeing it. Because transference involves feelings about the pastoral counselor, it can be embarrassing. It raises questions about the pastor's identity; therefore, that identity needs to be firm enough to allow the counselee to distort it. In ordinary social relations a person would try to ignore what was going on or attempt to minimize it. In supervision, however, I attempt to support students enough so that they will go against the natural tendency to respond to anxiety and go toward the counselee's feelings about him/her rather than to move away from it. If I, as pastoral counselor, become anxious, I can use this feeling as a signal that I am involved in some way and that I should attend to the transference. As a supervisor, my responsibility is to help students learn to use their anxiety and respond in this way.

Related to that anxiety and the ability to move toward it rather than away from it is the pastoral counselor's "inappropriate" importance to the counselee. One can estimate the maturity of a student as a pastoral counselor in terms of his or her willingness to be this important. Students who have difficulty learning this type of ministry consistently manage to ignore their importance to their counselees and to talk about something else. They can acknowledge the principle theoretically, but they fail to learn it experientially.

Another way of talking about the transference in supervision is one to which we have previously referred: the contrast between what's going on in the room and what's happening outside. This focus of supervision here is not so much on the counselor's importance to the counselee, but on the ways in which the issues of life outside the room can be brought inside. When things are going well in the counseling, what is going on "between us" becomes more important than what is going on "out there." Both pastoral counselor and counselee learn to look at their relationship for clues about life. Things can be seen in the room which simply cannot be seen outside. It is often much easier to experience and express anger toward the counselor for his or her apparent failure to provide emotional warmth for a counselee than it is to take that feeling directly to the real father. Moreover, when that feeling is expressed, we in the room have the luxury of looking at it and learning from it long after its expression. The parent who died years ago can, through the transference, be present again, and some of those things that were never said or even directly experienced can be experienced and set to rest.

Within the supervisory relationship, another thing is seen consistently in the student's effort to manage the transference. The first interpretations of the transference tend to be too abstract for the counselee to use. Or, again, in an effort to avoid the anxiety of that intense personal relationship, the inexperienced pastoral counselor may deny his or her responsibility to risk an interpretation by asking such a vague question as, "How do you feel about our relationship?" In more than fifteen years of counseling supervision, I have heard that question over and over again and have never heard a counselee who knew what to do with it. The general principles of interpretation in pastoral counseling belong to the next chapter. The point here is that effective interpretation of the transference must risk being concrete and personal, not vague comments about relationships. For example, "I've noticed that you always seem to move in your chair before you say something that in any way disagrees with me," or, "It's gotten easier for you to let me be important to you."

These are the kind of concerns that come up consistently in supervisory sessions with persons who are trying to learn pastoral counseling. Learning to manage the transference is like learning to ride a bicycle. The supervisee either has the feel of it and is doing it or is not doing it. There is not much in between. Once it has been learned, it can become less awkward and more graceful, but the basic learning is either present or not present. This assertion raises two important questions: (1) How does the learning of a specific practice, such as managing the transference, relate to pastoral counseling understood as the giving of oneself? and (2) How is learning to manage the transference relevant for a pastoral counselor who has decided to limit his or her practice to relatively short-term counseling?

With respect to the first question, students consistently challenge their supervisors on the issue of how learning to develop one's own style in counseling can be at all consistent with learning how to perform a specific task, such as, managing the transference. The supervisor at the same time seems to be saying to himself and to the student, "Be yourself; do what I tell you to do." At one level this raises the whole question of how a person acquires practical knowledge. At another level it represents the demand of our norm for pastoral counseling, relational humanness: be related, but don't lose your humanness in the process.

Coming to terms with these seemingly conflicting messages is the focus of the supervisory process. Within the context of a relationship that is pastoral—caring, but structured and accountable—the students are challenged to involve themselves in a specific action and then reflect and learn from it in the light of their whole being. How do I carry out this task as John Patton? And what does the doing of it contribute to what I am? The "action-being dialogue" does not resolve the conflict, but, within the context of a significant relationship, it makes it manageable. Unfortunately, even with the most effective supervisor the answer to the questions sometimes is: in the light of who I am, I cannot perform this particular task.

Some persons cannot learn to manage the transference or handle long-term relationships.

But how is the management of the transference relevant for the pastors who, for one reason or another have decided to limit their practice of pastoral counseling to relatively short-term relationships? It is less important in shorter relationships, because there are fewer ways to use the transference experience. However, it remains one of the more important elements in pastoral counseling. Pastors who can discipline themselves to listen and demonstrate understanding of what is being said can indeed perform a valuable service. Even in a one-session counseling experience, however, "the problem" is never just "out there." It is also in the room. The pastor who is in touch with the manifestations of transference phenomena, and who can make inferences from and sometimes interpretations of them is in a much better position to be useful to someone, regardless of how long the relationship may be. The pastor who comments to a first-session counselee, "I notice that when you ask me for anything you always seem to apologize. I wonder if that's the way you are with other people too," is dealing with the transference phenomenon. Some of the problem is being lived in the counseling room and it should be attended to as well as what the counselee says. Transference is resistance to the process as it is going on, but it is far more than that. It is a constant reminder to the pastoral counselor that the most important thing in the counseling process—the relationship—must be attended to first.

Countertransference

But what about countertransference reactions—the way my own feelings may distort the relationship with my parishioner or counselee? Robert J. Langs defines countertransference as:

> one aspect of those responses to the patient which, while prompted by some event within the therapy or in the therapist's real life, are primarily based on his past significant relationships;

basically, they gratify his needs rather than the patient's therapeutic endeavors.[18]

In a later work on supervision, Langs simplifies his definition by saying that countertransference is

all unconscious, pathological, and distorting fantasies and introjects which disturb the therapist's interaction and work with his patient.[19]

The central issue with respect to countertransference is being able to identify those feelings and fantasies that are disturbing to the relationship. Menninger is helpful at this point. Countertransference, he says, "is dangerous only when it is forgotten about."[20]

Some knowledge of the countertransference reaction can assist pastors, at all levels of training and experience, in dealing with the potential in all of us to kid ourselves. If, as I believe, my feeling response, disciplined by supervision, knowledge, and experience, is indeed the best thing I have to offer my counselees, then it is essential that there be an ongoing supervisory confrontation to enable the pastor to deal with countertransference feelings. Although it is possible to offer a useful and valid ministry without this, personal therapeutic experience is also essential for pastors who choose a ministry that involves them deeply with people.

The important thing, then, in dealing with countertransference reactions is the kind of self-awareness that comes through supervision, consultation, and personal psychotherapy. The concept of abstinence, as applied to oneself, is also helpful. The focus of the caring relationship is on the person cared for, and the many things that could gratify me—most of them relatively benign—must be kept secondary. My needs, however, although secondary, are an essential part of the humanness that I offer in relationship. They cannot, therefore, be hidden from the counselee under the guise of a false objectivity. My feelings are, in an important sense, what I am at a particular moment, and thus, what I have to give.

Recall the case of Joanne in the first chapter. Her feelings of sadness and grief put me in touch with my own. I did not become depressed, in the sense of being trapped in an experience I could not cope with. I simply allowed myself to feel with her the genuine sadness involved in the process of human life, and expressed my need to experience life along with her. In that moment, I was not aware of what I now understand as my unconscious or intuitive therapeutic concern. I wanted to say to her, following Freud, "What you are experiencing is not hysterical misery, not pathology, but 'common unhappiness.' "[21] To say that in words would have been like the irrelevant reassurance that we have heard so many times, "There, there, everything will be all right." It will be, but not if I disrespect the feeling and try to take it away prematurely. The message of reassurance will more likely be heard as I express my own humanness, my own feeling of pain, and say, by exemplifying it, "You are not the only one. Your pain is the sadness of being human."

The Lover Dimension

Whereas concepts from psychoanalytic psychotherapeutic theory can contribute significantly to the development of the parent dimension in pastoral counseling, it is the tradition of experiential psychotherapy that contributes most significantly to what I, with the help of Joanne, have called the "lover" dimension—the capacity to offer oneself in relationship in an open and genuinely human way. I am not saying that this dimension of the pastoral relationship is derived from experiential psychotherapy, but that what is inherent in pastoral counseling—understood in terms of the norm, relational humanness—can be further clarified and enriched by this view of psychotherapy. Psychoanalytic theory assists us in understanding the profound importance of developing the capacity to exemplify the *parent* dimension. Experiential theory encourages us to be a pastor by surrendering the very capacity which we have so painstakingly developed.

Experiential theory is not the same as, but does resonate with, that element in the picture of Christ which "did not count equality with God a thing to be grasped" but became fully involved in the experiencing of human life. Experiential psychotherapy, as Thomas P. Malone describes it "refers to those *experiences* occurring between or among two or more persons which increase the *capacity* of anyone of the participants to experience more of either his/her inner life or his/her living relationships to everyone and everything surrounding him/her." The experiential psychotherapist is:

> one who finds techniques and theoretical systems that are most congruent with his/her person, and so allow him/her the fullest and most feeling expression of their personality and character in relating to patients. The key concept is congruence. The congruence between the therapist's technique-system and his/her person allows the maximal personal participation in the relationship to the patient.[22]

"I bring myself to psychotherapy," says Richard Felder, "because I would be unwilling to try to proceed with psychotherapy on the basis of figuring out what the patient needs to hear and trying to say it convincingly. This would seem too artificial, and I would fail at it."[23]

Experiential therapy, according to John Warkentin,

> designates the therapist's goal: That the patient and therapist will *experience each other* in such a way that the patient benefits, and the therapist has the joy of being used both as a professional and as a person. . . . This experiencing is always in the present; however, the content of the interaction may be the history of the patient, his living outside, his transferences or a consideration of his choice in living.[24]

The term, "experiential psychotherapy,"[25] is associated not only with that group of therapists in Atlanta who were in practice with Carl Whitaker and John Warkentin, but it is also associated with many who formerly referred to their therapeutic orientation as "client-centered." Perhaps most influential among this group is Eugene Gendlin, a philosopher, who came into the study and practice of psychotherapy out of a conviction that "direct experiencing is 'implicitly' rich in meanings, but is never equitable to words or concepts. Experiencing is the organism's interaction with all the environment." Gendlin's present work is with experiential "focusing,"[26] a type of lay and professional training designed specifically to capture the elusive dimension of experiencing and, thus, improve the efficiency of the psychotherapeutic process and sometimes replace it.

The emphasis of experiential psychotherapy is pointedly expressed by Thomas P. Malone in his article, "Psychopathology as Non-Experience."

> Simply stated, the experiential dimension in psychotherapy hopefully gradually displaces and vitalizes the transferential. The clear implication of this is that the transferential or neurotic is a non-experience, and that health, in contrast, is being in the current flow of experience appropriately able to move easily with the changing realities of inner and outer worlds of experience. Lack of awareness of one's inner world and the inability to move easily with the ever-changing outer world, particularly the outer world of other persons, characterizes the neurotic or transferential.[27]

Malone shares with Walker Percy the concern for redeeming the "ordinary Wednesday afternoon."[28] He is skeptical of the lasting effect of weekend encounters, religious or secular, and believes that Gestalt fantasy breakthroughs "rapidly succumb to the realities of washing dishes." What people return to again and again "is their hunger for meaning in their ordinary experience. They seek the assurance that they can move into the flow of life, experiencing fully both their person and the other, as they move together in both space and time."[29]

This is Joanne's quest as well, and the "religious person" who has the discipline and emotional capacity to be a "father" (parent) can assist her in it as a "lover." In using that word because she did, I run the risk of being misunderstood. But I use it for emphasis and for identification with the love of Christ, which in one important sense may be understood as a full experiencing of all of life. It is sexual, but not physically so, because sexuality is part of the fullness of life. It was physical in Joanne's case only in the good-bye hug which she initiated at the end of the session. During the intensity of the experiencing there was no physical contact. The "lover" dimension of pastoral counseling is the fully experiential, rediscovered in relationship.

I have argued in this chapter that what heals in pastoral counseling is relationship and have attempted to describe the important dimensions of that relationship through the use of concepts from psychotherapy. Pastors do not have to practice psychotherapy for concepts from this discipline to be valuable in their practice of ministry. I have used the designation of the pastoral counselor, as "father" and "lover," in the case of Joanne as a device for interpreting the psychotherapeutic concepts and have suggested that they represent important dimensions of the pastoral counseling relationship. The dimensions may be thought of as dialectically or sequentially related. The exact relationship between them does not seem essential to the argument. What I have said throughout the chapter is intended to apply both to the work of parish ministers and to that of pastoral counseling specialists. All of what I have said is informed by the norm for pastoral counseling—relational humanness.

The power of this norm for the Christian pastoral counselor is in its identification with the person and work of the Christ. Persons do not have to be Christians to express relational humanness, but for Christians there is in Christ a revelation of what it means to be human and what it means to be in a relationship that inspires, informs, and corrects them. As a Christian pastoral counselor, whatever relational humanness I can express is deepened by the revelation of the Christ that both my counselee and I were created for neighbor-hood and that what we are about together is an expression of what we were created to be. My understanding of human pain and brokenness perhaps should include the material in the *Diagnostic and Statistical Manual of Mental Disorders,* but that knowledge is sobered and made less arrogant by the relational pain revealed by Father and Son in the cross. It is difficult for me to maintain my detachment when I remember and experience something of the loss experienced on both sides of that relationship. Nevertheless, the same event corrects my hopelessness. Some kind of healing is possible in spite of who we are—in spite of the limits of our humanity and our relationships. The Holy Spirit is the Christ of neighbor-hood and of the cross somehow alive again creating community where community seems impossible.

Humanness in relationship is not all we know or need to know about the Christ, but it is a dimension of his person and work which can most effectively illuminate and be illuminated by the ministry of pastoral counseling. The power of this norm has the practical implication of giving more meaning to my efforts to manage the transference as it appears with counselees. If the way things really are can somehow be seen in Christ's relational humanness for us, then it is easier for me to imagine neighbor-hood with some of the impossible people with whom I work. It is easier for me to tolerate the embarrassment of being somebody's grandmother and to allow someone to experience new hope from me even when I am not aware of having any. This kind of theological thinking places together the sublime and the ridiculous—the Christ event and my relationship to persons in pastoral counseling. My understanding of that event, however, is that in spite of the peculiarity of this combination, that's really the way it is supposed to be.

Chapter Eight

What Happens?—The Process of Pastoral Counseling

Stated simply, what happens in pastoral counseling is that people talk to each other. Or, actually, they learn to. At first they may just talk. I became aware of how much talking is not really talking to someone when I substituted for a colleague in leading a therapy group. I had sat in the group and listened without saying anything for about half an hour before I became aware that the group members were not talking to one another. A lot of words had been said, but as I reflected on what had happened thus far, I realized that no one had said anything to anyone else. It was as if each person was talking to the spaces between people rather than to another person.

No doubt the presence of a new leader had increased the anxiety of the group and reduced the effectiveness of their functioning together. In my presence, it was more difficult to be specific about anything, and the communication had become unfocused and general. They were not yet ready to be seen doing that very personal thing—talking to another human being. Shortly after becoming aware of this, I said to a woman who had just finished speaking, "Who were you talking to?" She looked surprised and said, "No one in particular, just to the group, I guess." The same thing continued with other group members until my calling attention to what was going on began to make a difference. With this kind of help from me, group members began to look at another person when they talked and, in connecting with that particular person, they seemed to become more related to other persons in the group.

Another experience comes from farther back in my memory. Some years ago, when I was chaplain at a children's hospital, I discovered that a number of parents who had spent a great deal of time at the hospital with a sick or dying child would come back long after the child had been discharged or had died. Sometimes they wanted to see a particular staff member who had been important to them during the child's illness. More often they seemed to be looking for something more intangible. Their comments went something like this: "Coming here brings back a lot of pain, but there was something we had here that we don't have any more. Life seemed deeper and more important. We were able to talk about serious things." Some of those parents were quite unsophisticated. They weren't quite sure what it was they were looking for, but it seemed to be a quality of life and a kind of communication that their ordinary life did not offer.

These incidents suggest two important things about what happens in pastoral counseling. The first suggests that the language of pastoral counseling is communication *to* someone. It is language understood in the context of a relationship. It is a relational language that becomes common to the two or more persons who use it for their exploration together. It is not a static, but a developing, language which creates nuances of meaning as the relationship progresses.

The second incident suggests that pastoral counseling uses, or moves toward using, a depth language that goes beyond the processing of information. It is a feeling language that is capable of expressing human pain, but something more than that. The discussion in this chapter, then, concerns the development of a relational story, with feeling, and with something more.

The talking to and talking deeply of pastoral counseling involve three interrelated dimensions: story, feeling, and meaning. A discussion of them and the way they appear in pastoral counseling make up the remainder of the chapter.

What heals in pastoral counseling is relationship, but the development of relationship, of neighbor-hood, involves telling stories, sharing feelings, and suggesting meanings.

An important part of what it means to be human is having a story, experiencing depth of feeling, and discovering meaning. Pastoral counseling is one of ministry's ways of communicating this.

To state the problem in a different way, what I am doing in this chapter is presenting a hermaneutics of pastoral counseling. Although a recent study by Charles Winquist[1] has made the concept of hermeneutics central in a theory of ministry, this way of thinking about pastoral care and counseling has been surprisingly slow to develop. I recall using the term "hermeneutics," as early as 1972 in a discussion on pastoral supervision and consultation.[2] More recently, I attempted to show how some principles drawn from the field of hermeneutics could be used to enrich the interpretation of case material in pastoral counseling.[3] My intent was to point out some of the similarities in the interpretation of documents and to interpret the "living human document."[4] Although in discussing what happens in pastoral counseling in terms of the interrelated dimensions of story, feeling, and meaning I am involved with hermeneutical theory, the focus of my concern is not so much theory as on the actual function of interpretation in pastoral counseling.

Telling Stories

The first type of interpretation to be discussed is the kind that assists a person in the discovery or rediscovery of his or her story. Humankind is presented in the Bible as existing as a part of history and in community. Persons are not isolated units moving from one experience to another. Normatively understood, they exist as a part of something. What the pastoral counselor sees, however, whether he or she practices ministry in a parish or counseling center, is many persons who have become cut off from their roots, their network of relationships, and their sense of direction. Without roots, relationship, and direction, they have difficulty telling their story. Often, they can only present a problem. The memory of who they are and where they are going is dim.

Ernest Schachtel, writing in the late forties, described the memory loss of adults as a result of cultural conditioning rather than, as Freud had suggested, of repression.

> It is not merely the repression of a specific content, such as early sexual experience, that accounts for the general childhood amnesia, the biologically, culturally, and socially influenced process of memory organization results in the formation of categories (schemata) of memory which are not suitable vehicles to receive and reproduce experiences of the quality and intensity typical of early childhood. The world of modern Western civilization has not had use for this type of experience.[5]

Adult memory, Schachtel continues, is much like the stereotyped answers to a questionnaire which can provide facts and dates but not much of the narrative connection between them. I described some of this in the discussion on the stereotyped answers I have received to the question, What hurts? in the chapter on diagnosis. Needless to say, the difficulty continues into the process of counseling after the evaluation process is completed. I have had occasion to say to a number of people during the process of pastoral counseling, "I think you flunked 'Show and Tell.' " This is a way of telling them that something important was left out of their childhood experience—that exciting business of a child of four or five being given an audience of his or her peers and one or more interested adults to tell and illustrate a story about *him* or about *her*. The process of pastoral counseling can be a "re-take" of that essential experience of "let me tell you what happened to me!" Hearing the story is hearing more than the problem. The problem is not ignored, but the process of hearing stories and more about the person puts the problem in perspective—seeing it along with the rest of life and with the lives of others. Stories help break through the isolation of being locked up in one's pain and the Elijah-like paranoia of "I, even I only am left."

Sheldon Kopp,[6] Sam Keen,[7] and others have affirmed the importance of story in psychology and psychotherapy. Ross Snyder[8] has done so in the context of theological education under the rubric of "phenomenologizing"—the recapturing of the basic phenomena of life. Larry Churchill has argued for the "primacy of stories over stages" in the death experience. In a fascinating critique of Kubler-Ross' stages or, rather, of "those of us who have taken her metaphors literally and ossified her 'stages' into lock-step movements," he argues that "the notion of story is essential if our understanding of the dying is to be commensurate with their experiences."[9]

A central problem in life is literalism, trying to make clear and distinct what is by nature multilayered and mysterious. The function of therapy for James Hillman, therefore, is acquainting persons with the fact that this is the way life is and involving them in the process of exploration.

> Therapy is one way we can revivify the imagination and exercise it again. Of course we have to go back to childhood to do this, for that is where our society and we each have placed imagination. Therapy has to be so concerned with the childish part of us (not for empirical developmental reasons) in order to recreate and exercise the imagination. The entire therapeutic business is this sort of imaginative exercise, and it picks up again the oral tradition of telling stories. Therapy is a restorying of life.[10]

"Successful therapy," says Hillman, "is . . . a collaboration between fictions, a revisioning of the story into a more intelligent, more imaginative plot." Hillman criticizes Freud's theory "because it fails poetically, as a deep enough, embracing enough, esthetic enough plot for providing dynamic coherence and meaning to the dispersed narratives of our lives. . . The patient is in search of a new story, or of reconnecting with his old one. . . The way we imagine our lives is the way we are going to go on living our lives. For the manner in which we tell ourselves about what is going on is the genre through which events become experiences. There are no bare events, plain facts, simple data."[11]

Hillman identifies Freud's method of interpretation with allegory and Jung's with metaphor. For Freud, the task was to translate the manifest into the latent, surface into depth. Free association was an attempt to secure material that could be translated from one to another by appropriate interpretation. For Jung, the metaphor of the patient's verbal production should not be translated. The latent and manifest exist side by side affirming different levels of existence. Both Freud and Jung, however, were concerned with the reconstruction of the human story, and it is this general concern that the pastoral counselor shares with them.

But how is this concern for story expressed in what happens in pastoral counseling? It is expressed through interpretation which helps connect or reconnect the apparently isolated events of our lives. And, as stated in the previous chapter, material from psychoanalytic psychotherapeutic theory can assist the pastoral counselor in carrying out this task. The contribution of the psychoanalytic tradition to what happens in pastoral counseling comes first of all in what the pastor can learn from the attitude of the analytically trained psychotherapist. Saul describes this attitude in the following way:

> The technique of analysis requires a double attitude on the part of the analyst. This fundamental split involves holding in abeyance the knowledge of background and nuclear dynamics while listening uninfluenced to the associations and integrating them only after the main theme revealed by the associations is understood. The analyst must see the main issues, the core of the dynamics, the central emotional constellation, the essential problem, the total personality and its history. But, at the same time and with the perspective of this insight, understanding, and knowledge, he must approach each session completely afresh, completely without preconception, listening with gentle curiosity to hear what will come up today, as though he never had seen the patient before.[12]

What can be learned from this passage which, in the context of Saul's book is about the technique of free association, is what Freud described as "a calm, quiet, attentiveness" in which the pastoral counselor learns to listen without jumping to conclusions. He or she looks for the commonalities and connections in what is said, but resists making interpretive generalizations too quickly. One of the dimensions of the counselee's "problem," whatever it is, can be at least partially corrected as he or she observes and learns from the pastoral counselor's openness to experience and his or her avoidance of quick explanations of profound life experiences. The relationship should gradually give the counselee enough security to collect data about his/her life without immediately having to do something about it.

The pastoral counselor can usefully adopt the psychoanalyst's attention to the ordinary—the assumption that through the data of ordinary life meaning can be found. It is not necessary to start with the extraordinary and apparently important events and feelings. The psychoanalytic assumption that everything is connected to everything else allows you to begin where you are. Because of this, even the most unimportant sounding things have potential meaning. One can begin the search anywhere and be attentive to the connections as they emerge. The psychoanalyst's use of the method of free association does not commend that method to the pastoral counselor, but it does commend that attitude. It can underscore the importance of hearing a person's story and of getting beyond the problem to the whole of life and the curious connection of human events.

Interpretation as Connection

Interpretation is the connector of events. I use the term in a different sense later in the chapter. Here my concern is to emphasize the important function of interpretation in *connecting* the events of a person's life into a narrative. As I noted earlier, Karl Menninger has suggested that intervention may be a better term than interpretation. He says:

> Interpretation is a rather presumptuous term. . . . I dislike the word because it gives young analysts the wrong idea about their main function. They need to be reminded that they are not oracles, not wizards, not linguists, not detectives, not great wise men who, like Joseph and Daniel, "interpret" dreams—but quiet observers, listeners, and occasionally commentators.[13]

With the attitude of which Menninger speaks, pastoral counselors can learn a great deal from the psychoanalytic concept of interpretation. To interpret, says Greenson, is

> to make conscious the unconscious meaning, source, history, mode, or cause of a given psychic event. This usually requires more than a single intervention. The analyst uses his own unconscious, his empathy and intuition, as well as his theoretical knowledge, for arriving at an interpretation. By interpreting we go beyond what is readily observable and we assign meaning and causality to a psychological phenomenon.[14]

How deep the pastoral counselor reaches into unconscious meanings is related to the context of the counseling and the training of the counselor. Broadly understood, however, interpretation is a means of enriching the counselee's concept of history—his/her own history—through suggesting a pattern previously unseen. The discernment of that pattern has been called, in the psychoanalytic literature, insight. It is the simultaneous identification of one's characteristic behavior pattern in one's contemporary life situation, the therapeutic relationship, and one's past life. The function of interpretation is to suggest connections among these dimensions of the life story. In the process of analysis, according to Menninger, the patient

> successively goes from aspects of the contemporary situation to the analytic situation, thence to related aspects of the childhood situation, thence to the reality situation and on around the circle in the same *counterclockwise* direction. This is typical, proper,

and correct in analysis. We have support for this proposition from Freud's general advice that analysis should proceed from the so-called surface to the so-called depth.[15]

Other psychoanalytically oriented psychotherapists refer to the type of interpretation that enables the patient to connect his/her present life situation, the transference, and past experiences as a "total interpretation."[16] Our concern here is not with a norm for psychotherapeutic interpretation but with the importance of these three dimensions in the counselee's life as they represent important concerns for the pastoral counselor. Being able to move among the three is important to the counseling whether it takes places in a parish or a pastoral counseling center. If the counselor is working with a parishioner, then the use of the counseling relationship will be limited, because transference manifestations will complicate other relationships in the parish with that person. The pastor can, however, help a parishioner see his or her contemporary situation in perspective by attempting to relate it to his or her history as this is informed by the pastor's observations of how he/she and the parishioner have been related in the parish.

The inability to facilitate movement from life situation to relationship with the pastoral counselor to past life and back again can make the counseling an endless repetition of the counselee's caughtness in "the problem." He or she has lost both past and future and has only an intolerable now. The counselee needs the perspective of the counseling relationship and of his/her history in order to achieve insight into the problem—whatever it is—and move beyond it. Although they may be used in certain cases of long-term pastoral psychotherapy, the techniques of free association and interpretation are less important in themselves than in what they represent. For most pastoral counseling, they represent a need to move beyond the problem to the story, so that the problem can be seen as only a significant feature of the story, not the whole story of that person's life.

Personal Myth and Symbol

Another useful way to think of the restorying process in pastoral counseling is in terms of personal myth and symbol. Myth, according to Mircea Eliade,

> narrates a sacred history. It relates an event that took place in primordial Time, the fabled time of our "beginnings." In other words, myth tells how . . . a reality came into existence, be it the whole of reality, the Cosmos or only a fragment of reality—an island, a species of plant, a particular kind of human behavior, an institution.[17]

John Dominic Crossan makes use of Claude Levi-Strauss' structural theory of myth and describes its primary function as "mediating irreducible opposites. . . . Myth has a double function: the reconciliation of an individual contradiction and, more important, the creation of belief in the permanent possibility of reconciliation."[18]

Extending these understandings of myth to the disconnected, storyless person whom we often see in pastoral counseling, the importance of personal myth and symbol become evident. The goal of the pastoral counselor is to help the counselee discover," I am not what I am just now. I came from somewhere." The process of pastoral counseling should be able to convey something like the identity-forming message of Deuteronomy, "Once you were no people; now you are God's people."

Many persons have lost touch with the "fabled time of their beginnings." This was true of Sally, some of whose story was presented in the first chapter. She was disconnected from a network of support. Like the children of Israel, she lived in a strange city. The "unfair" death of Aunt Rebecca suggested to her that she lived in an alien world, one which was essentially unfriendly. "I don't see how if there is a God, he could allow this kind of thing to happen. I don't know what I believe any more. Why bother living?" Sally continued. "Why work, why do anything?"

The pastoral counselor's task is to hear and be sensitive to

Sally's despair, as well as to look for her story and the possibility of her reconstructing a reconciling myth in the midst of an apparently unfriendly world. Although Aunt Rebecca was peculiar and Sally's father made fun of her, she "was always doing something for somebody else," and, as Sally put it, "She was there when I needed her. Whenever my mother wasn't there, it seemed like Aunt Rebecca was." And more than that, "Aunt Rebecca and I are the only ones who know how to make grandmother's caramel cake."

Even within these very few pieces of a story there are the makings of a personal myth. It might go something like this:

> Even though I am separated from the place I come from and feel disconnected and like "no people," I am reminded that I am like Aunt Rebecca. When I had no mother, she took me in and taught me family tradition—caring for people who need help, making cake, and growing violets. Even though she has died, some of her life lives on in me. She continues to help me know who I am. Death and estrangement are partly overcome by her life in me and my commitment to be like her and reach out to other people.

Sally's myth, implicit in the dialogue between us, is not the story of heroes and goddesses or of ancient times. Rather, it is the story of recent times and of an ordinary woman who can hardly be called the founder of anything—though, perhaps, there are some vital dimensions in her life. It is a personal myth that deals with only a "fragment of reality," but it does answer the question of where Sally came from and helps mediate between the "irreducible opposites," death and life. The task of the pastoral counselor is not to construct the myth, as I have done here for illustrative purposes. It is, instead, to use the connective function of interpretation to help the counselee restory her life and to become a part of something again.

The discovery of story in pastoral counseling contributes to the process in still another way—one that can be seen implicitly in what I have said thus far. It facilitates the development of relationship. The counselee, in telling the story, moves beyond his or her helplessness and the demand, "Take care of me!" The dependency need remains, the need for relationship, but it can be entered into with less desperation. Hearing different dimensions of a person's story enables the pastoral counselor to find things he or she can identify with, respect, and genuinely enjoy—all of which are necessary for a pastoral counseling relationship. I have been convinced for some time that it is impossible for me to be useful to anyone in the relational experience of pastoral counseling if I cannot respect, affirm, and genuinely care for them. Part of the early task of pastoral counseling, is finding a way to do this. One of the questions I have been hearing for years from persons who do not understand what pastoral counseling is about is, "How do you stand listening to people's problems all day?" I usually just smile and say, "It's not so bad," because I don't believe they would understand my real answer: "I don't listen to problems. I listen to stories."

Sharing Feelings

The second type of interpretation to be discussed here is that which assists persons in distinguishing between events and their response to them. The talking to and talking deeply of pastoral counseling involves recognizing and sharing feelings. Telling a good—a relationship-building—story requires the recognition that one's feelings about an event are a part of the event itself. Nevertheless, what happened and how one felt about the event need to be distinguished. As I noted earlier, many people cannot immediately answer the question, What hurts? Their feelings may be too painful or, because of the pain, they have pushed the feelings far enough away that they are no longer "felt." One of the values of an evaluation of a person's total life situation is that it places his or her pain in the context of a history. It also slows down the counseling process so that one does not have to move immediately into the affective dimension of life.

Walking around the problems and getting used to each

other before moving right in on that feeling of panic may be the best way to reduce the counselee's anxiety so that he or she can share that feeling. The tendency of all of us, however, is to continue to stay away from anxiety or any kind of intense feeling. Without supervision, consultation, or enough experience so that being with anxious persons is familiar territory, the pastoral counselor will continue to respond to content rather than feeling long after the appropriateness of the early caution about moving too quickly into feelings has passed.

Just as the runner in football may be coached to "run to daylight," rather than to follow the play as sketched on the chalkboard, the pastoral counselor should often hear from his/her suprvisor, "Run to affect." "Where is the feeling in all those words?" "What's going on inside that person as he talks about this?" This may be the part of technical training in pastoral care that most pastors have been able to glean from clinical pastoral education. If they have learned to respond more effectively to feelings, they have learned something that will continue to be useful in pastoral work.

It is important to respond to feelings, call attention to them, and reinforce their recognition. Because feelings can be embarrassing, they are often hidden in the midst of other communication. Certainly, the orderly process of social relationships requires that feelings be disguised and often not expressed. The socialization process is one that disguises and ritualizes our sexual and aggressive feelings and encourages us to do the same to others. The pastoral relationship, to be effective, however, must help persons sort out their feelings in a way that allows appropriate expression—honesty and directness in personal relationships and ritualization and disguise in those that are less personal. The phrase, which has become a cliche, "getting him in touch with his feelings," seems to me to be a part of the norm for pastoral care, particularly, for pastoral counseling.

Stated simply, pastoral counseling that has helped a person distinguish more effectively between his or her feelings and the facts or events of life has performed a valuable service if it does nothing else. Personal relationships are continually complicated by the failure to make that distinction. One of the most common examples is this: I am angry at you because you have not responded to me in the way I want you to. I am embarrassed by my feeling of rejection and my anger about it; therefore rather than sharing my anger as my own feeling, I will attack you, calling attention to what is wrong with you rather than what I fear is wrong with me.

I recall thinking that perhaps we had taught our children to untangle some of this when, after attacking my son verbally for something he had not done that I had expected him to do, he said to me, "Are you asking me to do something or just telling me how bad I am?" In spite of what I was doing then, I must have done something right in teaching him to call me to account about my own dishonesty with my feelings.

Virginia Satir in her books, *Peoplemaking* and *Making Contact*[19] has offered a great deal of practical help with this in a way that is usable for the average person. The communication theorists[20] with whom Satir was formerly associated at Palo Alto have offered further help at both the theoretical and the practical level. For example, the principle that communication is always a multi-level phenomenon in which there is both content and a message about the relationship of those communicating is continually useful in understanding and interpreting what is going on in a relationship.[21] Most consistently helpful in my learning to be responsive to feelings, however, are those therapists who have been associated with Carl Rogers or who have been identified as experiential psychotherapists—John Warkentin, Tom Malone, Eugene Gendlin.

In writing about a current view of client-centered therapy Eugene Gendlin, long associated with Rogers both at the University of Chicago and the University of Wisconsin, identified *listening* as the essence of client-centered therapy. The "two new additions" to client-centered therapy that Gendlin identifies are both clarifications of what is meant when listening is taken seriously. The first of these is *exact specificity* in the response to what the counselee has said about his/her feelings. Most client-centered responses have been, says Gendlin, "only round approximation." The client's distinctly felt experience, rather than being articulated, was obscured and deprived of its specific edges by such responding. Accuracy is most important as an aim of the therapist.[22]

The second "new addition" is the therapist's encouragement to the client to "check inside" to see whether the essence of the feeling has been grasped and stated. "Without this inner checking by the person listened to, there is no way to become exact, and no way to make really direct contact with what's there in the person."[23] It is too easy for the clients to give up getting in touch with their feelings; therefore an essential part of the therapeutic process is taking those feelings completely seriously by checking and rechecking to see that both parties in the relationship are in touch with what is going on[24] Gendlin continues:

> Years ago, I reformulated client-centered therapy from negative to positive, from don't rules, to *do* rules. The old rules were: don't ask questions, don't answer questions, don't say your own feelings, don't interrupt, and so on. I changed it to "Make sure you do say what you understand, and let that be checked out, so you stay in touch with the person. Given you do this, you can do anything else also." The therapist's own self-expressing, for example, is welcome, provided that the person is really listened to before, after, and continually.[25]

This is about as useful a piece of advice for pastoral counselors that I know of and is one that seems quite consistent with the norm of relational humanness. It is also consistent with John Warkentin's description of experiential psychotherapy[26] as participation in the psychotherapeutic relationship "with a disciplined sharing of ourselves."

> The ideal therapists bring a candor born of their own experience as a patient, a skill and wisdom learned in their training and living,

plus a willingness to commit themselves as instruments in the patients' effort.[27]

Warkentin quotes appreciatively a former colleague, Dr. Tom Leland, who at one time also served as the psychiatric consultant for our pastoral counseling service: "I sell the use of my eardrums for 50 minutes. My heart is not for sale, and will respond only to another heart." Experiential therapists, Warkentin continues,

> go beyond selling their time, wisdom, interviewing skill, and office space. We are not dealing with the therapist as merely a "doctor," "teacher," or "consultant." We are considering his emotional readiness to feel his own affection, his annoyance, and his many other feelings while in the presence of a patient.[28]

The experiential therapist "may offer himself to be almost as transparent as the patient hopes to be, and perhaps the therapist even serves as an example of this to the patient."

> It seems to me that this kind of personal relating with patients is possible only for those therapists who are growing people. The personal maturity of the therapist becomes of utmost importance in the question: "How valuable or usable am I to my patients?" . . . There is a joy in relating to growing people that has nothing to do with intellect. It is an adventurous journey of discovery. . . . This I seek with all my patients, with laughter, tears, tension, and sometimes disappointment. Such satisfactions make me willing to undertake the hard work and firm self-discipline which are essential to good therapy. I feel rich in the experiences afforded to me by those who come to share their lives with me.[29]

I have quoted at length from John Warkentin both because he is a kindred spirit from whom I have learned much and because his views help clarify what it means to "talk deeply" in pastoral counseling. It means feeling and experiencing deeply some of the pain and joy of life. It is, in my judgment, what happened in the interview with Joanne that was described in the first chapter:

> As she gradually calmed down, I reflected some of her feelings verbally, but mostly became aware of my own sadness. I don't

think at this point I knew what the sadness was about. It was clear to me that as she began to feel better, my own pain got worse. Although I was primarily aware of my own feelings, I was also aware that she was talking about my caring for her. I shared with her a fantasy that had come to me as she had moved up out of her despair and had been expressing herself in words. In my fantasy I had gone for supervision to a wise therapist/friend. Instead of presenting a case, I had put down my tape recorder and cried for forty-five minutes. I don't believe I shared this next reflection with her, although I am not sure, but it seemed that the reason for my tears was something about the sadness of life, the fact of death, and the inability of caring to take all the hurt away. I do remember that she asked me about my friend, and I told her briefly about how at several specific points in my life he had helped me. I cried openly, and Joanne smiled. The session ended with Joanne coming over, hugging me, and hoping I would feel better.

I discussed this incident earlier in terms of the "lover" dimension of the personal relationship. I present it here as an example of interpretation of life through the expression of feelings. It is a way of saying, "What we are experiencing now is an essential part of what life is about. I can best tell you about it by being it and sharing what I am experiencing with you." Perhaps most striking is Joanne's move from the despair she experienced earlier in the interview to her response to my sadness. As I cried she smiled. I doubt that it was necessary to say that this was not a technique to treat her depression, but the way things really were with both of us.

Suggesting Meanings

What happens in pastoral counseling is the telling of stories, the sharing of feelings, and something more. The something more is the suggestion of meaning, particularly theological meaning. It is the type of interpretation that not only suggests connections among the elements of the story, but also suggests what the story is all about.

That phrase, "suggesting what the story is all about," seems to me to be excitingly presumptuous. Even softening its impact with a qualifying word like, "suggesting" rather than using "proclaiming" or "announcing" only slightly lessens the presumptousness. And yet this is exactly what ministers are there for and trained to do. They do not have a corner on the market for story interpretation, but much of the education of the minister is directed toward this task.

Fortunately, this is not all the minister has been set apart for and trained to do. If it were, most of what I have said thus far would be irrelevant. Christian ministry is much more than verbal witness and interpretation, though it is, in my judgment inescapably that—even for the pastoral counseling specialist. The question is, How is such interpretation integrated into the total task of pastoral counseling so that neither the interpretation nor the ministry of pastoral counseling is obscured? Returning to the case of Sam and Sally may help us answer this question.

Recall that Sally began the session by sharing her feelings of despair. "Nothing's any better." As she is experiencing it, things are just as they were when the counseling began. Instead of responding directly to Sally's hopeless feeling, I pursued my curiosity in the light of my knowledge of Sally. The despair was placed in the context of having seen Sally move significantly beyond where she was when she and Sam began counseling. What's going on now may feel the same to her, but it is obviously different. Any response I make needs to be appropriate to the specific situation she is experiencing, not some general response to her feeling. She mentions her aunt's death but disclaims its importance. My curiosity about the discrepancy between her present feeling and the total counseling experience and my general understanding about the power of grief lead me to explore the death further.

What I do at this point in the interview is essentially the same as any pastoral care response to grief. I encourage the person who is grieving to talk about her loss. Sally is embarrassed by her grief, because it exposes her vulnerability to loss and pain. The success of the counseling thus far has helped her deny that. What she says in her despair, "Nothing's any better," I perceive as being untrue clinically, but Sally, without being aware of it, is speaking at a deeper level. Unconsciously she has re-experienced her vulnerability to the inevitable pain of life. In that sense, she is right. Everything is just the same. I use the relationship that has been established to live with her in that experience of her world's brokenness, explain a few things about grief, and encourage her to get more specifically into her pain about Aunt Rebecca. Sally finally affirms that in spite of the self-reliance and independence that are so important to her in coping with a difficult life, there are important times when she was dependent on her aunt. As she tells the story, she begins to let go the anger at herself for being so vulnerable.

She was in Aunt Rebecca's house. She wanted something of hers and took the violets. Aunt Rebecca could never get them to bloom; perhaps she can. She and her aunt were the only ones who knew how to make the caramel cake. Now the secret belongs to her alone. She relived the moment of eating the cake, affirmed how good it was to her, and agreed to use the secret (the mystery) which had been passed on to her and to share it.

For anyone who is intrigued by symbols or by the multi-level layers of meaning of which Hillman speaks, it obviously requires great restraint not to move in and "make something" out of what appears to be going on. I presented this case to a group of colleagues who saw a variety of options for interpretation which I had not seen for it is a piece of human experiencing that is "meaning-full." My interpretation was a "suggestion" about Holy Communion and that Sally might know more about what it means now. I did not say directly, "What you experienced was Holy Communion." I did not know that. I believed—and still do—that the interpretation should take place by my suggesting a symbol that was common to my experience. She had a choice what to do with it.

My other theological reflection on Sally's experience with Aunt Rebecca's death was that it revealed something about the sacrificial death of Christ and that unconsciously the way she talked about Aunt Rebecca grew out of her understanding of the story of Christ. She was better able to understand and experience Aunt Rebecca because of her faith in the Christ story and better able to experience the meaning of the Christ because of Aunt Rebecca. All of that seemed important even then, but my clinical judgment said to me that such an interpretation would be too "heavy" and intellectual, taking her away from the concrete richness of that experience. Theologically, my conviction was that if the Holy Spirit can operate only on an intellectual level and not on the unconscious or preconscious, then we're all in trouble. A person does not have to have a full intellectual grasp of what is essentially a religious experience for that experience to operate with power in his or her life. Had I found the words to give even a brief christological statement, I would have in all probability lost Sally and the way she was experiencing her world. My concern as pastoral counselor was to be a part of her world, not ask that she understand mine.

My task in the interiew itself was to interpret the event as it occurred with the symbols most likely to illuminate my counselee's experiencing without erasing the experience in favor of the symbols. In that moment of life, for Sally, the sacrificial death of Aunt Rebecca was more important than the sacrificial death of Christ. Had I de-emphasized the former in favor of the latter I would have diminished the meaning of both. The uniqueness of that experience had to be claimed in its fullness before it could be linked to any other event, even the Christ event. We must begin to perceive some of the meaning and importance of our own stories before as John Dunne has suggested, we can *pass over* to the story of Christ.[30]

Perhaps the most important thing that can be said about the type of interpretation of meaning which is most appropriate to pastoral counseling is that at its best it is metaphorical or parabolic. I can only suggest and hope that she who has ears will indeed hear. I can make what literary critic Phillip Wheelwright has called a "soft focus" on meaning and hope that my hearer will bring the meaning into sharper focus for herself. "There are meanings," Wheelwright continues, "which do not have definite outlines and cannot adequately be represented by terms that are strictly defined. Certain poetic utterances are obscure because the subject matter itself is too subtle and illusive to allow exact delineation or because one can produce an effect more fully by producing an ambivalent impression in the reader's mind."[31] Only in "language having multiple reference can the fully manifold, and paradoxial character of primordial mystery find fit expression."[32] What Wheelwright says about literature of this type seems directly relevant to interpretation of the meaning of the story in pastoral counseling.

The deeper experiences of a person's life, those that are "meaning-full" and those that connect a particular life with an affirmation of what life is about, cannot be interpreted as to their meaning in a heavy-handed, literal manner. They deserve a "soft-focused" response that offers a choice and, in many cases, a challenge. The paradigm for the latter may well be the parables of Jesus, which, according to Robert Funk,[33] leave the mind in sufficient doubt about their precise application in order to tease it into active thought. The parable is not closed until the hearer is "drawn into it as a participant." Or, as Charles Hackett, following Merleau-Ponty, has suggested[34] the parable does not communicate a piece of information with regard to reality, but deforms reality as habitually perceived. It functions in many ways like a painting that calls attention to a particular part of life, sometimes distorts it, and, in doing so, calls attention to a dimension of it that is usually not perceived. That deformation of a particular part of reality may raise questions about and suggest meanings for a particular person and/or all of life.

The recent literature on the interpretation of parables is a valuable resource for the pastoral counselor. The parable and certain types of intervention in pastoral counseling serve a similar function—creating an image that challenges and involves the hearer, thus making possible choice about changing his or her way of life. "The surface function of parable," according to Crossan,

> is to create contradiction within a given situation of complacent security but, even more unnervingly, to challenge the fundamental principle of reconciliation by making us aware of the fact that *we made up the reconciliation*. Reconciliation is no more fundamental a principle than irreconciliation. You have built a lovely home, myth assures us: but, whispers parable, you are right above an earthquake fault.[35]

Many personal myths are discovered to be on shaky ground. Sally's myth about her self-sufficiency had functioned well in the familiar environment of her hometown, but it began to crumble in a strange city. My insistence on her telling me about her aunt was not parabolic in its confrontative sense, but it did serve to undermine the view that she had handled her life on her own and was not really a part of a family. More clearly in the parabolic mode was an interpretation to a young man who had a personal myth that he had to be better than his father. The father had divorced Tom's mother when Tom was in his early teen yars, so Tom had structured much of his life to be better than Dad. In one counseling session, he found himself struggling with his feelings of depression and his disloyalty to a girl upon whom he had become quite dependent, but to whom he was no longer attracted.

Pastoral
Counselor: Well, it looks like you're no better than your father after all.

Tom: What do you mean?

P.C.: I thought that was what your sadness was about. I was sitting here thinking about that part of the Elijah story where he says, "O Lord, take away my life; I am no better than my fathers." He seemed to be pretty depressed too.

Tom: You mean that's the way I've lived my life?
P.C.: What do you think? Have you got a better explanation for your sadness?
Tom: I guess not.
P.C.: You may have to learn to live with being like him.

Clinical material seldom offers an exact illustration of the principle it is intended to illustrate, but even pulled from its experiential context, this incident has the parabolic quality of demonstrating an attack on a personal myth. Much of the story dimension of the parable is implicit, but the function of indirect confrontation and involvement is carried out in the interaction. This way of thinking about pastoral counseling needs a much fuller treatment than can be given here, but perhaps enough has been said to be suggestive of the possibilities.[36]

Comparing interpretation in pastoral counseling to the kind of intervention presented in the parable should remind the pastor that this type of interpretation is ineffective when it is explained. The most uncomfortable times I have in supervision are those in which I hear a student make an apparently useful interpretation, have it seem to fall on deaf ears, and then try to explain it or improve on it. Whatever power an interpretation had is lost as it is explained and each metaphorical element given a literal meaning. One of the most obvious illustrations of this is in the New Testament is the explanation of the parable of the sower in Mark 4:14-20[37] which, in me at least, stirs up an image of anxious disciples, worried about not enough ears hearing, robbing the parable of its power by trying to improve on it. Pastoral counselors do the same thing when they try to explain their interpretations.

> **P.C.:** Sally, what you experienced in Aunt Rebecca's house was like Holy Communion because you ate something she had made as an act of remembering her. That was what I meant in saying that you might know more now about what Holy Communion means.

I find it embarrassing just to imagine doing that, and yet I hear similar explanations again and again from pastors who have difficulty saying something and letting it go.

The literature on biblical interpretations that is relevant for pastoral counseling, however, is much broader than that which focuses on the parables. Robert Tannehill's study of the "forceful and imaginative" language of the Synoptic Gospels may have as many implications for interpretation in pastoral counseling as for the interpretation of the New Testament. Features of the New Testament accounts which Bultmann, in his effort to demythologize, dismissed as ornamental, are presented by Tannehill as quite important. Forceful and imaginative language affects the lens through which one images reality.

> Our visions of self and world can be sinful or redemptive, false and crippling or a guide to fullness of life. False and crippling visions often hold us in bondage because we cannot imagine anything else. . . . Plain speech is good for communication within established interpretations of the world but it bypasses the imagination and so has little power to change these fundamental interpretations.[38]

Look at this fragment of personal myth from a young woman in her late twenties who had an identical twin: "I guess I always felt that Tracie was the one who did the living and I was one who stood around and watched." This is indeed a "crippling vision." It illustrates powerfully the need to find *a new way of seeing* which can lead to increased depth and richness in one's personal and communal life.

The experience of a new way of seeing is something much more powerful than the term, "insight," as it is used in the psychoanalytic tradition, can capture. It involves the opening up of choices previously unseen and a challenge, sometimes a demand, that they be acted on. The term most often associated with this experience is "reframing," which grew out of the system and communication theory on which most family therapy is based. Quite literally it means putting what one sees in a different frame or context, enlarging the perspective or system so that elements not previously seen as related to the focal point may be seen and experienced as related. Reframing "breaks the illusory frame inherent in any world image, and theory reveals that what appeared unchangeable can indeed be changed.[39]

Although I have difficulty integrating some of the structural and systematic interventions described in the family-therapy literature into my understanding of the pastoral relationship and with the norm of relational humanness, I do believe the concept of reframing is an important one in broadening and enriching the meaning of interpretation in pastoral counseling. The serious work of systematically relating the theoretical implications of family-therapy literature and the power of religious language to induce change, however, will have to wait until a later time.

If an interpretation of any kind is a good one, it involves what Seward Hiltner and Carl Rogers taught us years ago, knowing the other person's world so well that any message emerges from within it rather than being imported from the outside. Rogers avoided the concept of interpretation for reasons similar to those voiced by Menninger earlier in the chapter. It can—if it comes without a "soft focus"—sound like pontificating rather than responding. Rogers sought to discover the internal frame of reference of the client. I prefer to think of response to the counselee or the best interpretations as emerging from the community that has developed between the pastor and his counselees. A good interpretation is born out of a good relationship.

I have been asked many times by students in clinical pastoral education, pastoral counseling supervision, or by pastors in conferences on pastoral care such a question as this, "If you take this point of view of saying only things that come out of the relationship, how do you *bring in* Christ?" The too quick answer, which does not take the question seriously enough, is, "You don't have to bring him in, he's already there." True, perhaps, but it does not seem to me to deal adequately with the necessary visibility of ministry, which includes appropriate usage of the language of faith. For a counselee unlike Sally, who had been referred by a pastor and talked freely about her faith, the language, not the Christ, is brought into the counseling relationship.

The issue for the pastoral counselor is to be able to hear the invitations to use Christian symbols when they come. If the counseling relationship has moved to the point where the particularities of who I am as a person are as important as what the counselee needs me to represent, then I have the freedom to use whatever symbols come most naturally to me to describe the depth of human experience. Before that time, I feel bound to respond almost wholly to the counselee's world with very little brought in from outside. With respect to the invitation, the young woman who became uncomfortable when I asked her about her religious history and later dreamed that her own high school principal was asking her to recite Bible verses, had given me an invitation to continue to raise religious questions with her. If I "bring Christ in" verbally, I do so with a "soft focus," or in a way that gives the counselee a choice of meanings. I can speak briefly of what Christ has meant "to men of old times" but the counselee will have to decide what Christ can mean to him or her.

What happens in pastoral counseling is that people learn to talk *to* one another. They learn to talk more deeply about meanings that are important to them. They develop a relational language which serves to deepen the experience that the counseling offers to all of them—the individual, couple, and counselor. In the process of the counseling, they become better storytellers—perhaps discoverers of their myth —learning to tell their stories with feeling rather than making generalizations about their problems. They discover in relationship—by talking to one another—that there is more than one way to look at things. The most important things have a soft focus. They can be understood in depth but not with full clarity. The most important things have to do not only with the content of the story, but also with what the story is all about.

I have said very little about dreams and their place in pastoral counseling, so perhaps this chapter and the book can best be concluded with two dreams from counselees which, without losing their "soft focus," speak rather eloquently on what pastoral counseling is all about. Mark and Mary came to see me originally for help with Mary's depression over their retirement in a strange city. After the depression had been lifted, or had been identified as part of the normal sadness of life, they continued to come to share their vision and dreams. Mary told me one of her dreams. She was supposed to meet a friend on a train going to McKeesport (which is where she grew up). She missed the train, but instead of taking the next train to McKeesport, she went on another train, not knowing where it was going. In doing so, she went past McKeesport and got off at the stop beyond, which was called, as she remembers it, "New Port or New Port News or something like that."

The symbol of the new city in Mary's dream, one which is beyond the home city, is reminiscent of many biblical symbols. The fact that it occurred in her dream and that she, Mark, and I had an opportunity to explore it together confirmed for all of us that at seventy she was no longer in despair, as Walker Percy might say, but "onto something."

Another dream from another person tells more of what our stories are all about. A woman of fifty-five came to me because of her bondage to anger against her husband who had disappointed her. She had lived for him and the children. Now the children had left home, and he had let her down. She had been good, done the right things, but it had not worked out. As we moved through a turning point in the counseling process, she brought in a dream. In the dream she came home to discover that her house had been burglarized and precious antiques had been stolen. She was upset and angry and quickly called the sheriff to apprehend the thief. She waited for some time, but the sheriff did not come. Instead, a truck drove up to her door, and men brought in other valuable possessions of hers which she had had in storage and had forgotten about.

One does not have to "explain" either of these dreams to know that when things go well, this is what happens in pastoral counseling.

Notes

Introduction

1. John Patton, "Pastoral Counseling Comes of Age," *The Christian Century* 97 (March 4, 1981): 229-31.

2. Morris Taggart, "The A.A.P.C. Membership Information Project," *The Journal of Pastoral Care* 26 (December 1972): 219-44.

3. Robert R. Holt, "Summary and Prospect: The Dawn of New Profession," in *New Horizon for Psychotherapy,* ed. Robert R. Holt (New York: International Universities Press, 1971), pp. 312-411.

4. Seward Hiltner, "The American Association of Pastoral Counselors: A Critique," and Howard J. Clinebell, "The Challenge of the Specialty of Pastoral Counseling," *Pastoral Psychology* 15, (April 1964): 8-28.

5. Gaylord B. Noyce, "Has Ministry's Nerve Been Cut by the Pastoral Counseling Movement?" *The Christian Century,* 95 (Feb. 1-8, 1978): 103-6, 114.

6. Paul Tillich, *Systematic Theology,* vol. 1 (Chicago: University of Chicago Press, 1951), p. 59. The extent to which Tillich's norm is fully correlative and mutually corrective among all the component elements of systematic theology is debatable. Can the norm be modified by the elements with which it is in dialogue? My own point of view is that a norm can be both corrected and enriched through such dialogue without losing its normative character.

7. *Ibid.,* p. 54.

8. *In Quest of a Church of Christ Uniting: An Emerging Theological Consensus* (Princeton, N.J.: Consultation on Church Union, 1976), p. 35.

9. Cf. Carroll A. Wise, *Pastoral Psychotherapy: Theory and Practice* (New York: Jason Aronson, 1980).

10. Complete standards for certification in pastoral counseling may be obtained from the American Association of Pastoral Counselors, 9508A Lee Highway, Fairfax, Virginia 22031.

Chapter One

1. Peter Hodgson, *Jesus—Word and Presence: An Essay in Christology* (Philadelphia: Fortress Press, 1971), pp. 40, 42-43, 44.

2. Hans W. Frei, *The Identity of Jesus Christ* (Philadelphia: Fortress Press, 1975), p. 87.

3. Hans Küng, *On Being a Christian* (Philadelphia: Fortress Press, 1975), p. 87.

4. Langdon Gilkey, *Message and Existence: An Introduction to Christian Theology* (New York: The Seabury Press, 1979), p. 182.

5. *Ibid.*, pp. 182, 183, 185.

6. Jürgen Moltmann, *The Crucified God* (London: SCM Press, 1974), pp. 149, 243.

7. *Ibid.*, p. 245. Cf. also the further development of this theme of suffering love considered from both sides of relationality in Moltmann's *The Trinity and the Kingdom* (New York: Harper & Row, Publishers, 1981), particularly pp.21-83.

8. Moltmann, *The Crucified God*, p. 277.

9. Gilkey, *Message and Existence*, pp. 181-82.

10. Jürgen Moltmann, *Theology of Hope* (New York: Harper & Row, Publishers, 1967), p. 211.

11. *Ibid.*, p. 213.

12. Jürgen Moltmann, *The Passion for Life* (Philadelphia: Fortress Press, 1978), p. 24.

13. Karl Barth, *The Doctrine of Creation*, vol. 3 Part II, *Church Dogmatics* (Edinburgh: T. & T. Clark, 1960), p. 207.

14. *Ibid.*, pp. 220, 222-23, 228, 243.

15. *Ibid.*, pp. 250, 252, 259, 263, 267, 273, 285.

16. This interview was previously published in *Pastoral Psychology*, 29 (3) (Spring 1981): 160-62.

17. This interview was previously published in *The Journal of Pastoral Care*, 25 (3) (September 1981): 160-62.

Chapter Two

1. Urban T. Holmes, III, *The Priest in Community* (New York: The Seabury Press, 1978), pp. 158-59.

2. Talcott Parsons, *Social Structure and Personality* (London: The Free Press, Collier-MacMillan, 1964), p. 261.

3. Erving Goffman, *The Presentation of Self in Everyday Life* (New York: Doubleday/Anchor Press, 1959), p. xi.

4. J. L. Moreno, ed., *The Sociometry Reader* (New York: The Free Press), p. 80.

5. Cf. Barth's discussion of visibility as an essential characteristic of humanity, *The Doctrine of Creation*, pp. 250-52.

6. This can be seen in the standards for clinical pastoral education available through the Association for Clinical Pastoral Education, 475 Riverside Drive, New York, N.Y. 10017, both in the current standards and in previous editions, such as 1968. Discussions of the issue can also be seen in the proceedings of the conferences on clinical pastoral education published during the late fifties and sixties, some of which are still available through the A.C.P.E. office and others in theological libraries.

7. Eric Partridge, *Origins: A Short Etymological Dictionary of Modern English* (New York: MacMillan, 1958), p. 612.

8. Erik H. Erikson, *Childhood and Society,* 2nd ed. (New York: W. W. Norton & Co., 1963), pp. 251-54.

9. Cf. Frederich Buechner's artistic rendering of this in *The Book of Bebb* (New York: Atheneum Publishers, 1979), particularly in *Lion Country,* the first of the four novels included in this collection. Cf. also Heije Faber's image of the hospital chaplain as a clown in *Pastoral Care in the Modern Hospital* (Philadelphia: The Westminster Press, 1971), pp. 81-88.

10. Cf. J. Robert Nelson, *The Realm of Redemption* (London: The Epworth Press, 1951), pp. 160-72.

11. Tillich, *Systematic Theology,* vol. 3 (1963), pp. 163, 165, 153.

12. Cf. Tillich, *Systematic Theology,* vol. 3 pp. 149-216.

13. Here I am using my terminology rather than Tillich's and drawing out what seems to me to be clear implications of his position.

14. Cf. Paul Tillich, "The Theology of Pastoral Care" (address delivered at the National Conference of Clinical Pastoral Education, Atlantic City, November 9, 1956) in *Clinical Education for the Pastoral Ministry, Proceedings of the Fifth Conference on Clinical Pastoral Education,* ed. Ernest E. Bruder and Marian L. Barb (Washington, D.C.: The Advisory Committee on Clinical Pastoral Education, 1958), pp. 1-6. John H. Patton, "A Theological Interpretation of Pastoral Supervision," in *The New Shape of Pastoral Theology,* ed. William B. Oglesby, Jr. (Nashville: Abingdon Press, 1969), pp. 234-47.

15. Paul Tillich, *Theology of Culture,* ed. Robert C. Kimball (New York: Oxford University Press, 1959), pp. 203-8.

16. Theodore W. Jennings, "On Ritual Knowledge," *The Journal of Religion* (April 1982): 118-19.

17. D. MacKenzie Brown, *Ultimate Concern: Tillich in Dialogue* (New York: Harper & Row, Publishers, 1965), pp. 145, 161.

18. Tillich, *Systematic Theology,* vol. 3, p. 112.

19. Seward Hiltner, *Preface to Pastoral Theology* (Nashville: Abingdon Press, 1958), pp. 46-50.

20. Carl R. Rogers, *On Becoming a Person* (Boston: Houghton Mifflin Co., 1961), pp. 39-58.

21. An example of a popular skill training approach may be found in Robert Carkhuff's *The Art of Helping: A Guide for Developing Skills for Parents, Teachers, and Counselors* (Amhurst, Mass.: Human Resource Development Press, 1973). See also Carkhuff's *Practice and Research,* vol. 2 of *Helping and Human Relations: A Primer for Lay and Professional Helpers* (New York: Holt, Rinehart & Winston, 1969), Allen Ivey, *Microcounseling: Innovations in Interviewing Training* (Springfield, Ill.: Charles C. Thomas, Publishers, 1971), or Robert Bolton, *People Skills* Englewood Cliffs, N.J.: Prentice-Hall, 1979).

22. Probably the most valuable discussion of this model is still Thomas Klink's "Supervision" in Charles R. Feilding et al., *Education for Ministry* (Dayton, Ohio: American Association of Theological Schools, 1966), pp. 176-217. Cf. also John H. Patton, "A Theological Interpretation of Pastoral Supervision," in *The New Shape of Pastoral Theology,* pp. 234-47.

23. Robert Coles, *Erik H. Erikson: The Growth of His Work* (Boston: Little, Brown & Co., 1970), pp. 165-66.

24. Hans W. Frei, *The Identity of Jesus Christ* (Philadelphia: Fortress Press, 1975), p. 37.

25. In a provocative article, "Awakening Consciousness: The Psychological Reality in Christ-Consciousness," *Review and Expositor,* 76 (Spring 1979), Edward E. Thornton attempts to broaden the concept of pastoral identity beyond its usual association with the ordained ministry and with psychological ego identity by describing it as "an insatiable appetite for the Presence of God." The *pastoral* for Thornton denotes an awakening soul, alive to the Holy Spirit and thus involved in an internal dialogue which goes beyond introspection to awe and wonder at life and God.

26. Bernard Cooke, *Ministry to Word and Sacraments: History and Theology* (Philadelphia: Fortress Press, 1976), p. 197.

27. Tillich, *Systematic Theology,* vol. 2 (1957), p. 141, 139.

28. Frei, *The Identity of Jesus Christ,* pp. 45, 126, 127.

29. Patton, "A Theological Interpretation of Pastoral Supervision," pp. 242-46.

Chapter Three

1. Gibson Winter, "The Pastoral Counselor Within the Community of Faith," *Pastoral Psychology,* 10 (November 1959): 26-30.

2. Tillich, *Systematic Theology,* vol. 3, p. 165.

3. *The Book of Worship for Church and Home* (Nashville: The United Methodist Publishing House, 1964), p. 325, 50.

4. John Patton, "Condition and Covenant," *The Journal of Pastoral Care,* 32 (June 1978); 73-75.

5. For a brief note on consultation in an article devoted primarily to supervision, cf. John H. Patton and John Warkentin, "A Dialogue on Supervision and Consultation," *The Journal of Pastoral Care,* 25 (September 1971): 165-74. Although I disagree with his basic contention that consultation can be an alternative to supervision, Henry Adams' article in the same issue of *The Journal of Pastoral Care,* (pp. 157-64), "Consultation: An Alternative to Supervision," presents a useful consultative model. The literature of organizational development can also contribute to the understanding of pastoral consultation. Cf., for example, *Interpersonal Peacemaking: Confrontations and Third Party Consultation* (Reading, Mass.: Addison-Wesley Publishing Co., 1969). I have been influenced in my understanding of consultation by my former colleagues at the Atlanta Psychiatric Clinic and Center for Personal Growth who have several unpublished papers on consultation in psychotherapy.

6. John H. Patton, "The Pastoral Care of Pastors," *Christian Ministry,* 11 (July 1980): 15.

7. Tillich, "The Theology of Pastoral Care," p. 1.

8. Barth, *The Doctrine of Creation,* Part II, vol. 3, p. 263.

9. Quoted in Perry LeFevre, *The Prayers of Kierkegaard* (Chicago: University of Chicago Press, 1956), pp. 129-30.

Chapter Four

1. I avoid using the *term,* "patient," to describe persons receiving pastoral counseling because of its associations with medical practice and the general idea of an active professional doing something to a passive recipient of treatment. I find the concept of *patienthood,* in the sense of willingness to see one's need of help, as a useful one. It is the *concept* of patienthood that I am using in relation to Don Smith.

2. Sheldon Kopp, *Back to One: A Practical Guide for Psychotherapists* (Palo Alto, Calif.: Science and Behavior Books, 1977), p. 27.

3. John Patton, "Harry Stack Sullivan's Expert in Interpersonal Relations," *Journal of Religion and Health,* 9 (April 1970): 162-70.

4. Seward Hiltner, *Pastoral Counseling* (Nashville: Abingdon-Cokesbury Press, 1949).

5. Carl R. Rogers, *Client-Centered Therapy* (Boston: Houghton Mifflin Co., 1951).

6. Charles Truax and Robert Carkhuff, *Toward Effective Counseling and Psychotherapy: Training and Practice* (New York: Aldine Publishers, 1967).

7. Eugene T. Gendlin, *Focusing,* rev. ed. (New York: Bantam Books, 1981).

8. *Ibid.* See also Eugene T. Gendlin, "Client-Centered and Experiential Psychotherapy," in *Innovations in Client-Centered Therapy,* eds. David A. Wexler and Laura North Rice (New York: John Wiley & Sons, 1974), pp. 216-26.

9. Carl R. Rogers, *On Becoming a Person* (Boston: Houghton Mifflin Co., 1961). See particularly "To Be That Self Which One Truly Is," pp. 163-82.

10. The counselee may be uncertain of holding his/her own with the spouse present, may want to ventilate feelings about a particular incident, or feel that he/she must protect the spouse from what he or she feels. All of these are legitimate concerns, but are, I believe, less important than securing the optimum conditions for the counseling.

Chapter Five

1. The literature that has influenced me most includes: Murray Bowen, *Family Therapy in Clinical Practice: Collected Papers of Murray Bowen* (New York: Jason Aronson, 1978); Ivan Boszormenyi-Nagy and Geraldine M. Spark, *Invisible Loyalties* (New York: Harper & Row, Publishers 1973); Augustus Y. Napier and Carl A. Whitaker, *The Family Crucible* (New York: Harper & Row, Publishers, 1978); Virginia Satir, *Conjoint Family Therapy* (Palo Alto, Calif.: Science and Behavior Books, 1967); and Paul Watzlawick, *The Language of Change* (New York: Basic Books, 1978).

2. G. Ernest Wright, *The Biblical Doctrine of Man in Society* (London: SCM Press, 1954), p. 26.

3. Walter Brueggemann, "Covenanting as Human Vocation," *Interpretation* 33 (April 1979): 120.

4. See critique of premarital counseling literature in Theron S. Nease, *Premarital Pastoral Counseling Literature in American Protestantism, 1920-1971: A Descriptive and Evaluative Study of Family Models with*

Implications for Pastoral Care (Ann Arbor, Mich.: University Microfilms, 1973) and the theological critique of some of the marriage enrichment literature in Jasper N. Keith, "A Model for a Pastoral Care Ministry with Seminarian Couples," (S.T.D. diss., Columbia Theological Seminary, 1979).

5. This section is adapted from John Patton, "A Pastoral Perspective on Marriage and Family Counseling," *The Journal of Pastoral Care* 33 (March 1979): 38-43.

6. Ivan Borzormenyi–Nagy's concept of "invisible loyalties" may, in my opinion, apply to marriages as well as to parent-child relationships.

7. John Warkentin, "Marriage—The Cornerstone of the Family System," in *Family Dynamics and Female Sexual Delinquency,* ed. Otto Pollak and Alfred S. Friedman (Palo Alto, Calif.: Science and Behavior Books, 1969), p. 8.

8. Note Murray Bowen's concept of triangles, *Family Therapy in Clinical Practice,* pp. 478-80. I am using the concept in a positive sense. Rather than being "triangled in" by the tension in the marital relationship, the pastor takes the initiative and "triangles" himself/herself into the system in order to be more in control of the process.

9. Kahlil Gibran, *The Prophet* (New York: Alfred A. Knopf, 1923), p. 15.

10. An example of this may be seen in the recommendation of Gordon L. Bolte, "A Communications' Approach to Marital Counseling," in *Couples in Conflict,* ed. Alan S. Gurman and David G. Rice (New York: Jason Aronson, 1975), p. 335.

> During the first few conjoint sessions, the counselor may wish to take an inactive role, allowing each individual to present his or her version of the problems. The diatribe that often results is seldom beneficial per se, but it should provide the counselor with valuable information regarding the communication patterns of the couple.

My point of view, in contrast, is that it's not worth it, and it does nothing to build the relationship between the pastoral counselor and each member of the couple.

11. See, for example, Charles Stewart's *The Minister as Marriage Counselor* (Nashville: Abingdon Press, 1970); William J. Lederer and Don D. Jackson, *The Mirages of Marriage* (New York: W. W. Norton & Co., 1968); and Frank Bockus, *Couple Therapy* (New York: Jason Aronson, 1980).

12. Herbert A. Otto, ed., *Marriage and Family Enrichment: New Perspectives and Programs* (Nashville: Abingdon Press, 1976). See also Keith, *A Model for a Pastoral Care Ministry,* and Gerald J. Desobe, *Marriage Communication Labs: Perceptual Changes and Marital Satisfaction* (Ann Arbor, Mich.: University Microfilms International, 1978).

13. Virginia Satir, *Making Contact* (Millbrae, Calif.: Celestial Arts, 1976). This is the book I often give to couples to help them understand the communication process.

14. Pastors unfamiliar with family therapy literature are encouraged to make use of some of the references here and in the bibliography in Stewart's *The Minister as Family Counselor.*

Chapter Six

1. Committee on Nomenclature and Statistics of the American Psychiatric Association, *Diagnostic and Statistical Manual,* 2nd ed., (Washington, D.C.: American Psychiatric Association, 1968), and Task Force on Nomenclature and Statistics et. al., *Diagnostic and Statistical Manual,* 3rd ed. (Washington, D.C.: American Psychiatric Association, 1980).

2. Paul W. Pruyser, ed., *Diagnosis and the Difference It Makes* (New York: Jason Aronson, 1976); *idem, The Minister as Diagnostician* (Philadelphia: The Westminster Press, 1976).

3. Walker Percy, *The Last Gentleman* (New York: Farrar, Straus and Giroux, 1966), p. 353.

4. I base this statement on my own experience and that of my colleagues. I believe that it can be demonstrated by a fairly simple research design which samples the experience of pastoral counselees in several settings.

5. Paul Horgan, *Things as They Are* (New York: Farrar, Straus and Giraux, 1964, p. 1.

6. Peter L. Berger and Thomas Luckman, *The Social Construction of Reality* (New York: Doubleday/Anchor Press, 1967), p. 183.

7. *The Book of Common Prayer* (New York: The Church Pension Fund, 1928), p. 6.

8. *The Book of Common Prayer* (Proposed) (New York: The Church Hymnal Corporation and The Seabury Press, 1977), pp. 41-42.

9. William James, *The Varieties of Religious Experience* (New York: The New American Library, 1958), p. 26.

10. Carl R. Rogers, *Client-Centered Therapy* (Boston: Houghton Mifflin Co., 1951), p. 29.

11. Sheldon Kopp, *Everyone Wants to Be Special,* audiotape (Chicago: Human Development Institute).

12. Percy, *The Last Gentleman,* p. 354.

13. See the discussion of the languages of diagnosis in the essay by Karl Menninger and Paul W. Pruyser, "Language Pitfalls in Diagnostic Thought and Work," in *Diagnosis and the Difference It Makes* (New York: Jason Aronson, 1977), pp. 11-28, which extends the understanding of diagnosis far beyond its popular meaning as classification. See also Seward Hiltner's essay in the same volume, "Toward Autonomous Pastoral Diagnosis," pp. 175-94.

14. Roy Schafer, *Language and Insight* (New Haven: Yale University Press, 1978).

15. James Hillman, "The Fiction of Case History," in *Religion as Story,* ed. James B. Wiggins (New York: Harper & Row, Publishers, 1975), p. 140.

16. Edgar Draper, George G. Mayer, Zane Parzen, and Gene Samuelson, "On the Diagnostic Value of Religious Ideation," *Archives of General Psychiatry,* 13 (September 1965); 202-7.

17. Harry Stack Sullivan, *The Psychiatric Interview* (New York: W. W. Norton & Co., 1954), pp. 61-62.

18. Richard D. Chessick, *The Technique and Practice of Intensive Psychotherapy* (New York: Jason Aronson, 1974), pp. 95-98. See also Ralph

R. Greenson, *The Technique and Practice of Psychoanalysis* (New York: International Universities Press), pp. 45-48.

19. Virginia Satir, *Conjoint Family Therapy* (Palo Alto: Calif.,: Science and Behavior Books, 1964), p. 1.

20. John Patton, "The Pastoral Counselor as Specialist Within Ministry," *Pastoral Psychology* 29 (Spring 1981): 165-66.

21. Pruyser, *The Minister as Diagnostician*, pp. 60-79.

22. See William B. Oglesby, *Referral in Pastoral Counseling*, rev. ed. (Abingdon Press, 1978).

Chapter Seven

1. It should be evident to the reader that I am using the term, "parent" in a positive sense, in contrast to the negative way in which the term is used in transactional analysis.

2. John Patton, "The Necessary Tension Between Pastor and Layman," *Christian Advocate* (November 13, 1969); 7-8.

3. Ralph R. Greenson, *The Technique and Practice of Psychoanalysis* (New York: International Universities Press, 1967), pp. 151-52.

4. See John Patton, "Harry Stack Sullivan's 'Expert in Interpersonal Relations,' " *Journal of Religion and Health* 9 (April 1970); 162-70.

5. Greenson, *The Technique and Practice of Psychoanalysis*, p. 108.

6. *Ibid.*, p. 210.

7. *Ibid.*, p. 212.

8. Sigmund Freud, "Lines of Advance in Psychoanalytic Therapy," *Works*, standard ed. 17, (1919): 162.

9. Sidney Tarachow, *An Introduction to Psychotherapy* (New York: International Universities Press, 1963), p. 14.

10. Freud, "Lines of Advance in Psychoanalytic Therapy," p. 163.

11. Greenson, *The Technique and Practice of Psychoanalysis*, p. 222.

12. American Association of Pastoral Counselors, *Handbook* (Washington, D. C., n.d.), pp. 7-8.

13. James Dittes, *The Church in the Way* (New York: Charles Scribner's Sons, 1967).

14. Freud, "The Dynamics of Transference," *Collected Papers*, vol. II (London: Hogarth Press, 1924), p. 316.

15. Karl Menninger, *Theory of Psychoanalytic Technique* (New York: Basic Books, 1958), pp. 104, 105-7.

16. See for example Richard D. Chessick, *Technique and Practice of Intensive Psychotherapy* (New York: Jason Aronson, 1974) pp. 192-201; Greenson, *The Technique and Practice of Psychoanalysis*, pp. 76-150; and Menninger, *Theory of Psychoanalytic Technique*, pp. 99-123.

17. As with the references on resistance, I do not claim that those presented here are necessarily the most important. They happen to be those that I have used most frequently with pastoral counseling students. See for example Menninger, *Theory of Psychoanalytic Technique*, pp. 77-84; Leon J. Saul, *Psychodynamically Based Psychotherapy* (New York: Science House, 1972), pp. 305-26; and Greenson, *The Technique and Practice of Psychoanalysis*, pp. 151-89, 224-325.

19. Robert J. Langs, *The Supervisory Experience* (New York: Jason Aronson, 1979), p. 77.

20. Menninger, *Theory of Psychoanalytic Technique*, p. 90.

21. Joseph Breuer and Sigmund Freud, *Studies in Hysteria* (first published in 1895) trans. A. A. Brill (Boston: Beacon Press, n.d.), p. 232.

22. Thomas P. Malone, "Introduction," *The Roots of Psychotherapy*, Carl A. Whitaker and Thomas P. Malone (Reprint, New York: Brunner/Mazel Publishers, 1981), pp. xxiv, xxviii.

23. Richard E. Felder, "The Use of Self in Psychotherapy," in *Counseling and Psychotherapy*, ed. Dugald S. Arbuckle (New York: McGraw-Hill, 1967), p. 102.

24. John Warkentin, "Experiential Psychotherapy: A Contrast to Rational-Emotive Psychotherapy," *Journal of Contemporary Psychotherapy* 8 (Spring-Summer, 1976): 30.

25. My knowledge of experiential psychotherapy has come through supervision in client-centered therapy at The University of Chicago and through association with the Atlanta Psychiatric Clinic both as a patient and a staff member. Alvin R. Mahrer in his recent book describes experiential therapy much more broadly:

> As I read the scene, there is no single experiential psychotherapy. There is a family of experiential psychotherapies, more or less sharing a common humanistic-existential theory of human beings, and, at the same time, developing and refining various ways of using the common experiential axis of psychotherapeutic change.
> *(Experiential Psychotherapy: Basic Practices/*[New York: Bruner/Mazel, 1983], pp. 47-48).

26. Eugene T. Gendlin, "Client-Centered and Experiential Psychotherapy," in *Innovations in Client-Centered Therapy*, ed. David A. Wexler and Laura North Rice, (New York: John Wiley & Sons, 1974), p. 227. *Idem, Focusing* (New York: Bantam Books, 1981).

27. Thomas P. Malone, "Psychopathology as Non-Experience," *Voices* 17 (Summer 1981): 85.

28. Walker Percy, "The Delta Factor," in *The Message in the Bottle* (New York: Farrar, Straus & Giroux, 1975), p. 4.

29. Malone, "Psychopathology as Non-Experience," p. 86.

Chapter Eight

1. Charles Winquist, *Practical Hermeutics: A Revised Agenda for Ministry* (Chico, Calif.: Scholars Press, 1980).

2. John H. Patton and John Warkentin, "A Dialogue on Supervision and Consultation," *The Journal of Pastoral Care* 25 (September 1971): 169.

3. John Patton, "Clinical Hermeneutics: Soft Focus in Pastoral Counseling and Theology," *The Journal of Pastoral Care* 25 (September 1981): 157-68.

4. This phrase of Anton Boisen has become part of the ideology of the pastoral care movement. See Edward E. Thornton, *Professional Education for Ministry* (Nashville: Abingdon Press, 1970), pp. 55-71.

5. Ernest Schachtel, "On Memory and Childhood Amnesia," in *A Study of Interpersonal Relations*, ed. Patrick Mullahy (New York: Hermitage Press, 1949), p. 9.

6. Sheldon Kopp, *If You Meet the Buddha on the Road, Kill Him!* (Palo Alto, Calif.: Science and Behavior Books, 1972).

7. Sam Keen, *To a Dancing God* (New York: Harper & Row, Publishers, 1970), particularly pp. 84-105.

8. Ross Snyder, "What Is It All About?" in an issue of the *Chicago Theological Seminary Register* entitled "Becoming Consciousness" 62 (April 1972): 1-2; plus articles by other authors illustrating the theme.

9. Larry R. Churchill, "The Human Experience of Dying: The Moral Primacy of Stories over Stages," *Soundings* 62 (Spring 1979): 24-37.

10. James Hillman, "The Fiction of Case History: A Round," in *Religion as Story*, ed. James B. Wiggins (New York: Harper & Row, Publishers, 1975), p. 168.

11. *Ibid.* pp. 140, 132, 138, 146.

12. Leon J. Saul, *Psychodynamically Based Psychotherapy* (New York: Science House, 1972), pp. 179-80.

13. Menninger, *Theory of Psychoanalytic Technique*, p. 129.

14. Greenson, *The Technique and Practice of Psychoanalysis,* p. 39.

15. Menninger, *Theory of Psychoanalytic Technique*, pp. 147-51.

16. Saul, *Psychodynamically Based Psychotherapy*, pp. 259-60.

17. Mircea Eliade, *Myth and Reality* (New York: Harper & Row/Torchbooks, 1963), pp. 5-6.

18. John Dominic Crossan, *The Dark Interval* (Niles, Ill.: Argus Communications, 1975), pp. 56-57.

19. Virginia Satir, *Peoplemaking* (Palo, Alto, Calif.: Science and Behavior Books, 1972); *Making Contact* (Millbrae, Calif.: Celestial Arts, 1976).

20. For example, Paul Watzlawick, *An Anthology of Human Communication* (Palo, Alto, Calif.: Science and Behavior Books, 1964); Paul Watzlawick, Janet Helmick Beavin, and Don D. Jackson *Pragmatics of Human Communication* (New York: W. W. Norton & Co., 1967); and Don D. Jackson, ed., *Communication, Family, and Marriage; Human Communication*, vol. 1, and *Therapy, Communication and Change: Human Communication*, vol. 2 (Palo Alto, Calif. Science and Behavior Books, 1970).

21. Watzlawick, *An Anthology of Human Communication*, p. 3.

22. Gendlin, "Client-Centered and Experiential Psychotherapy," pp. 211-46, 214.

23. *Ibid.,* p. 215.

24. Gendlin, *Focusing,* is an extension of the client-centered emphasis on listening into a specific technique for assisting persons in discovering their pre-verbal experiencing.

25. Gendlin, "Client-Centered and Experiential Psychotherapy," p. 219.

26. See also Mahrer, *Experiential Psychotherapy: Basic Practices.*

27. John Warkentin and Elizabeth Valerius, "Seasons in the Affairs of Men," in *What Makes Behavior Change Possible?* ed. Arthur Burton (New York: Brunner/Mazel Publishers, 1976), p. 172.

28. Warkentin, "Experiential Psychotheraphy: A Contrast to Rational-Emotive Psychotherapy": 32-33.

29. *Ibid.,* p. 33.

30. John S. Dunne, *A Search for God in Time and Memory* (New York: Macmillan Co., 1967), pp. IX-XI.

29. *Ibid.*, p. 33.

30. John S. Dunne, *A Search for God in Time and Memory* (New York: Macmillan Co., 1967), pp. IX-XI.

31. Phillip Wheelwright, *The Burning Fountain: A Study in the Language of Symbolism* (Bloomington: Indiana University Press, 1954), pp. 62-64.

32. Phillip Wheelwright, "Poetry, Myth and Reality," in *The Language of Poetry,* Allen Tate (New York: Russell and Russell, 1960), p. 15.

33. Robert Funk, *Language, Hermeneutic and the Word of God* (New York: Harper & Row, Publishers, 1966), pp. 133-62.

34. Charles D. Hackett, *Hermeneutical and Homiletical Implications of Merleau-Ponty's Theory of Linguisticality* (Ann Arbor, Mich.: University Microfilms, 1976), pp. 158-75.

35. Crossan, *The Dark Interval,* p. 57.

36. Charles Gerkin's forthcoming book linking hermeneutical theory and pastoral care should contribute significantly to the exploration of this area.

37. According to Norman Perrin in *Jesus and the Language of the Kingdom,* (Philadelphia: Fortress Press, 1976), p. 101, "it is to Jeremias above all other that we owe our present ability to reconstruct the parables very much in the form in which Jesus told them." The allegorizing interpretation of the parable of the sower, in Jeremias' view was "added as the parable was transmitted in the early Christian communities. Allegorization was the favorite method of reinterpretation of the parables of Jesus."

38. Robert C. Tannehill, *The Sword of His Mouth* (Missoula, Mont.: Scholars Press, 1975).

39. Paul Watzlawick, *The Language of Change* (New York: Basic Books, 1978), p. 120. The entire book deals in one way or another with this issue.

Index